P9-CDS-611

GARDENING
WITHOUT
A GARDEN

GARDENING
WITHOUT
A GARDEN

·

GAY SEARCH

DK

A DK PUBLISHING BOOK

•

Project Editor Emma Lawson
Project Art Editors Gurinder Purewall, Emma Boys
US Editor Ray Rogers
Designer Darren Hill
Managing Editor Stephanie Jackson
Managing Art Editor Nigel Duffield
Production Controller Sarah Coltman
DTP Designer Jason Little

Senior Managing Editor Krystyna Mayer
Senior Managing Art Editor Lynne Brown

•

First American Edition, 1997
2 4 6 8 10 9 7 5 3 1

Published in the United States by
DK Publishing, Inc.
95 Madison Avenue
New York, New York 10016

Copyright © 1997
Dorling Kindersley Limited, London
Text copyright © 1997 Gay Search

Visit us on the World Wide Web at
http://www.dk.com

All rights reserved under International and Pan-American Copyright
Conventions. No part of this publication may be reproduced, stored
in a retrieval system, or transmitted in any form or by any means,
electronic, mechanical, photocopying, recording or otherwise,
without the prior written permission of the copyright owner.
Published in Great Britain by Dorling Kindersley Limited.

Library of Congress Cataloging-in-Publication Data

Search, Gay.
    Gardening without a garden / by Gay Search. – 1st American ed.
    p.   cm.
    Includes index.
    ISBN 0–7894–1457–0
    1. Container gardening.   I. Title
SB418.S43 1996
635.9'86 --DC20   96–38278
                                            CIP

Reproduced by Colourscan, Singapore.
Printed and bound by Star Standard Industries, Singapore.

CONTENTS

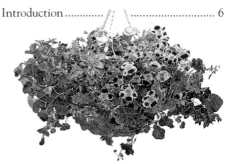

WALLS, STAIRS, AND ENTRANCES

SMALL SPACES

WINDOWLEDGES

CREATIVE PLANTING

CONTAINER AND PLANT CARE

PLANTER'S GUIDE

INTRODUCTION

One of the most exciting developments in gardening has been the surge of interest in growing plants in containers, with an increasing number of people realizing the enormous pleasure to be had, not simply from appreciating a finished display, but also from creating and maintaining the arrangement. In a small outside area, where available space is limited to a patio, balcony, or windowledge, gardening in a container provides a welcome opportunity to develop a green thumb. A small group of pots can also form a portable garden for those who know that they will soon be moving. In addition, containers can be used in a garden to bring living color right up to a building, or can feature plants that would not thrive in local soil conditions or survive during winter without protection. Like any form of gardening, planting in containers can be as simple or as sophisticated as your taste and horticultural confidence dictates, or your budget will allow. The aim of this book is to encourage you to be adventurous with your planting designs. There is no reason why you must limit yourself to using only annual bedding plants, for example, which last for just one season. Try featuring a tree in a tub, shrubs in a windowbox, or even a rose in a hanging basket. These plants will not thrive indefinitely in such confined conditions, but trees and shrubs that have outgrown their pots can be passed on to family and friends who have gardens. Or, perhaps by the time they are ready to transplant, you will have acquired a garden of your own.

ASSESSING A SITE

The characteristics of the proposed site for a display need to be determined before you choose plants and, to a lesser extent, a container. Consider whether parts of the site are in direct sun, part or full shade, or if the area is exposed to strong winds – plan carefully so that you can determine which plants will thrive

USING SHRUBS
A standard, evergreen viburnum underplanted with ivy and tulips in a Versailles-style tub makes a stylish display for a shady spot.

CREATING EYE-CATCHING DISPLAYS
A low-growing groundcover rose makes an eye-catching show in a hanging basket. Together with trailing annuals in similar pastel tones, it forms a shapely ball of flowers.

where. If you live in a mild climate, decide whether an area is sheltered enough to provide necessary protection for tender plants and terracotta pots from frost damage.

PLANNING FOR ALL SEASONS

A planted-up container will always take center stage. If you have a limited number of pots, it makes little sense to grow plants that will provide only a few weeks of glory. And, when space is at a premium, there are no out-of-the-way corners to hide a plant that is past its best. Plan an arrangement to give a long season of interest – a "skeleton" planting of evergreens with seasonal flower color from annuals or bulbs, for example, can look wonderful throughout the year. It is worth remembering that, while flowers can be spectacular, they seldom give as prolonged a show as foliage.

SELECTING A CONTAINER

The range of containers that is now available is extensive and diverse. Although terracotta, stone, and hardwood (from a renewable source) are attractive materials, plastic has really come of age. Containers made

DECORATING CONTAINERS

A quick and easy decorative finish, such as a layer of tiles, a mosaic, or a paint effect, can transform an ordinary plastic or wooden container into something strikingly original.

from this material are strong, lightweight, and inexpensive; some imitate natural materials; others are unashamedly synthetic.

Improvisation adds to the impact of an arrangement, and objects such as wicker baskets, copper cylinders, and galvanized trashcans can be transformed into eye-catching containers. Alternatively, give an inexpensive container an individual touch with a durable, decorative finish.

STYLING A GROUP

An arrangement is complete when a harmonious marriage between plants and container is achieved. These should complement each other in style, color, size, and shape: an elaborate planting design is highlighted by a simple container, and vice versa. Mixing colors can often be a question of taste, but succeeds when shades either contrast or combine. The sizes and shapes of plants and their container should also be considered so that the finished arrangement has a satisfying, visual balance.

Finally, the display can be placed in its proposed site. With regular maintenance your plants will remain healthy and attractive – a pleasure to behold.

MAINTAINING PLANTS

Looking after plants in containers and keeping them vigorous and healthy is comparatively easy, with your efforts yielding almost instant results.

UNDERSTANDING PLANT NAMES

Each plant may have a number of different names, a botanical name (written in italics) and several common names. For example, *Centaurea cyanus* is the botanical name for the plant often called a cornflower. A plant may be known by many common names that, in other countries, refer to different plants, creating scope for confusion. In order to ensure that a plant is correctly identified, it is essential that its botanical name is used, and not just its familiar, common name. Using universally accepted botanical names enables gardeners everywhere to identify plants accurately.

DEFINING THE PARTS OF A NAME

Genus
This first part of a name identifies the group of related species to which a plant belongs. Example: *Juniperus*.

Species
The second part of a name indicates a distinct group of plants within the genus. A genus can contain one or many species. Example: *Juniperus communis*.

Subspecies, varieties, and cultivars
This part of a name identifies plants that differ somehow from the species. If these differences occur in cultivation, the plant is known as a cultivar. Example: *Juniperus communis* 'Gold Cone'. If these differences occur in the wild, the plant is known as a true variety (var.). Example: *Juniperus communis* var. *montana*.

Hybrid
Indicated by "×", these plants are the offspring of two species in the same genus. They are given a different name from their parents. Example: *Juniperus* × *media*.

HOW TO USE THIS BOOK

The aim of this book is to help you to create and maintain a container garden. Beginning with inspirational planting designs, grouped according to their preferred location with ideas for alternative combinations, this section offers specific advice for planting up each display and keeping it in peak condition. This is followed by suggestions for designing with and selecting plants, covering such issues as matching a planting design to a specific site, and achieving a visually pleasing display. A comprehensive section on care includes tips on constructing, decorating, and looking after containers, as well as advice on basic routine tasks for maintaining plants, such as watering, feeding, propagating, pruning, and training. The book concludes with an informative index to the plants featured in the book, detailing their particular features and characteristics.

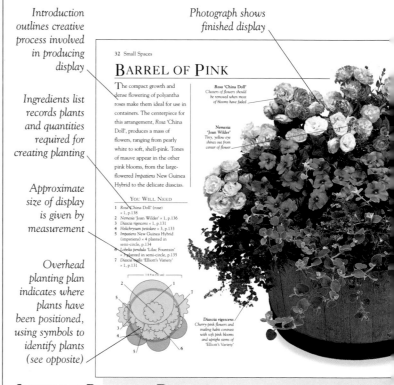

Introduction outlines creative process involved in producing display

Photograph shows finished display

Ingredients list records plants and quantities required for creating planting

Approximate size of display is given by measurement

Overhead planting plan indicates where plants have been positioned, using symbols to identify plants (see opposite)

32 Small Spaces

BARREL OF PINK

The compact growth and dense flowering of polyantha roses make them ideal for use in containers. The centerpiece for this arrangement, *Rosa* 'China Doll', produces a mass of flowers, ranging from pearly white to soft, shell-pink. Tones of mauve appear in the other pink blooms, from the large-flowered *Impatiens* New Guinea Hybrid to the delicate diascias.

YOU WILL NEED
1 *Rosa* 'China Doll' (rose) × 1, p.138
2 *Nemesia* 'Joan Wilder' × 1, p.136
3 *Diascia rigescens* × 1, p.131
4 *Helichrysum petiolare* × 3, p.133
5 *Impatiens* New Guinea Hybrid (impatiens) × 4 planted in semi-circle, p.134
6 *Lobelia pendula* 'Lilac Fountain' × 4 planted in semi-circle, p.135
7 *Diascia vigilis* 'Elliott's Variety' × 1, p.131

Rosa 'China Doll'
Clusters of flowers should be removed when most of blooms have faded

Nemesia 'Joan Wilder'
Tiny, yellow eye shines out from center of flower

Diascia rigescens
Cherry-pink flowers and trailing habit contrast with soft pink blooms and upright stems of 'Elliott's Variety'

INSPIRING PLANTING DESIGNS

The sections *Walls, Stairs, and Entrances, Small Spaces,* and *Windowledges* are divided by location and feature original plantings in a variety of containers, combining plants that have been chosen for their forms and textures as much as for their colors. These displays encompass different climates, seasons, and conditions, and are easy to duplicate or adapt.

Symbols indicate each plant's ideal conditions and hardiness

Plants are listed alphabetically, by botanical name

PLANTER'S GUIDE

The comprehensive *Plant Index* contains easily accessible information on all the plants featured in the book. The color, shape, and season of each plant is included, with symbols indicating correct growing conditions.

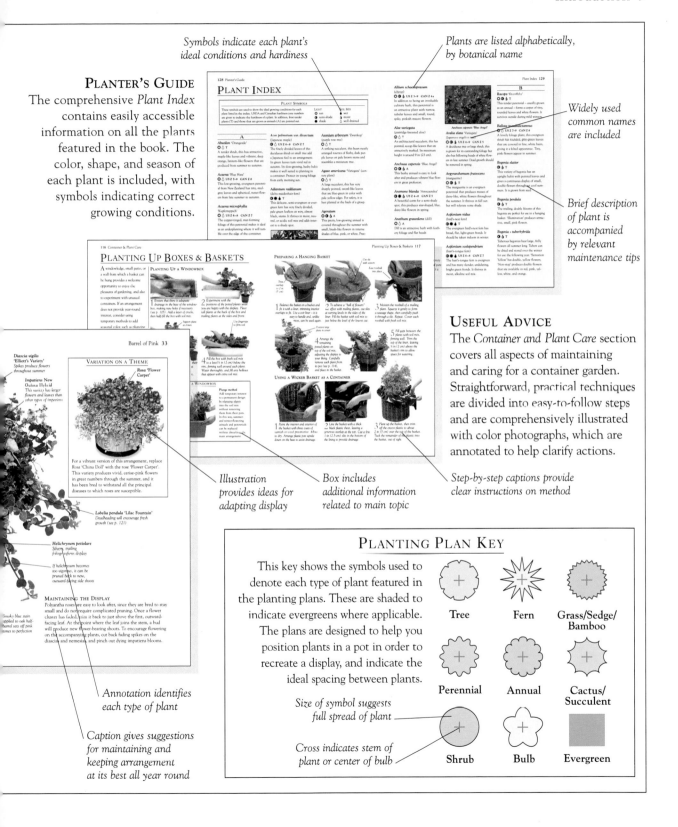

Widely used common names are included

Brief description of plant is accompanied by relevant maintenance tips

USEFUL ADVICE

The *Container and Plant Care* section covers all aspects of maintaining and caring for a container garden. Straightforward, practical techniques are divided into easy-to-follow steps and are comprehensively illustrated with color photographs, which are annotated to help clarify actions.

Illustration provides ideas for adapting display

Box includes additional information related to main topic

Step-by-step captions provide clear instructions on method

Annotation identifies each type of plant

Caption gives suggestions for maintaining and keeping arrangement at its best all year round

PLANTING PLAN KEY

This key shows the symbols used to denote each type of plant featured in the planting plans. These are shaded to indicate evergreens where applicable. The plans are designed to help you position plants in a pot in order to recreate a display, and indicate the ideal spacing between plants.

Size of symbol suggests full spread of plant

Cross indicates stem of plant or center of bulb

Tree Fern Grass/Sedge/Bamboo

Perennial Annual Cactus/Succulent

Shrub Bulb Evergreen

WALLS, STAIRS, & ENTRANCES

•

LEVELS OF PLANTING
A variety of terracotta pots and their
plants is casually arranged at different
heights on these steps, complementing
the informality of the setting.

A warm welcome can be extended to visitors by
decorating a main entrance with pots, windowboxes, and hanging baskets that are spilling over with
flowers and foliage. Planting designs and containers,
carefully chosen to complement the style of the house,
will bring life and color to a doorstep. Pot holders can
be hung from a painted trellis to liven up a wall, and
containers can be positioned on a flight of stairs to
introduce color and texture to a dull or shady area.

INVITING DOORWAY
The plain brick walls of this shady
entrance are brought to life with
a planting design of pink flowers
and shining green foliage.

FORMAL PLANTING

There are few things more effective than topiary for creating a formal entrance. Here, variegated standard hollies have been trained into eye-catching globes. The colors of their green-and-cream leaves are echoed by the plain, dark green leaves of *Hedera helix* 'Pittsburgh', the cream-colored dwarf *Narcissus* 'Jenny', and the white *Hyacinthus orientalis* 'L'Innocence'. These have been planted in a pattern that emphasizes the formality of the arrangement.

YOU WILL NEED

(quantities for one container)

1 *Hedera helix* 'Pittsburgh' (ivy)
  × 4, p.133
2 *Ilex aquifolium* 'Argentea Marginata'
  (English holly) × 1, p.134
3 *Hyacinthus orientalis* 'L'Innocence'
  (hyacinth) × 4, p.134
4 *Narcissus* 'Jenny' (daffodil)
  × 12, p.135

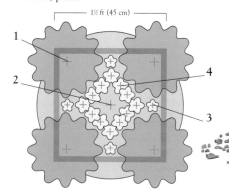

1½ ft (45 cm)

Ilex aquifolium 'Argentea Marginata'
Variegated leaves of holly are evergreen

Holly may produce bright red berries in autumn

*Foliage that reverts
to plain green
should be removed
immediately*

**MAINTAINING
THE DISPLAY**
Position the holly in sun
or semi-shade to retain the
variegation of its leaves. Trim
its branches regularly with
pruners to keep the globe in
a neat, bushy shape. When the
flowerheads of the daffodils
begin to fade, feed the dying
foliage to ensure a good
flowering next year. Cut the ivy
back in spring if its vigorous
growth becomes untidy.

*Standard shape
is maintained
by rubbing off
any new shoots
on trunk*

**Narcissus
'Jenny'**
*Daffodils should be
deadheaded as they
finish flowering*

**Hyacinthus
orientalis
'L'Innocence'**
*Bulbs planted in
autumn produce
ivory-white,
fragrant flowers
in spring*

*In summer,
hyacinths can
be replaced with
creamy-white,
scented stocks*

**Hedera helix
'Pittsburgh'**
*Ivy softens
container edges
and provides
color in winter*

*Straight-sided,
wooden
container
complements
formality of
planting*

FIERY RED TRELLIS

A large mass of one variety of plant can make a greater impression than a mixed planting, as demonstrated by this arrangement of the trailing balcony geranium, *Pelargonium* 'Fire Cascade', with its brilliant scarlet flowers. Sturdy, metal holders secure the simple, terracotta pots to a diamond trellis, painted black for dramatic impact. Hanging pots onto a painted or stained wooden trellis is an effective way of livening up a dull expanse of wall, especially if you use bold colors to blend or contrast with the planting design.

YOU WILL NEED

1   *Pelargonium* 'Fire Cascade' (geranium)
    × 8, p.136

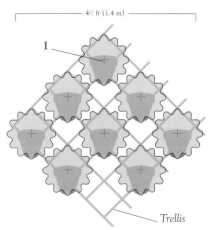

4½ ft (1.4 m)

1

Trellis

MAINTAINING THE DISPLAY

Position geraniums in a warm, sunny place to ensure a long flowering season. In a frost-free setting, these plants can remain outside all year round, but in cold areas, bring them indoors before the first frost. Replace them with winter-flowering *Viola × wittrockiana* (pansies) in a bright, single color such as yellow, orange, or blue.

Leaves are fleshy and ivy-shaped

Pelargonium 'Fire Cascade'
In hot weather, geraniums in small pots should be watered twice daily

Flowers are produced from early summer to late autumn

Small terracotta pots have been used to reduce weight

Dead flowerheads should be pinched out where stalk meets stem

Semi-ripe cuttings can be taken for next year (see p. 122)

FLOWERS BY THE BUCKETFUL

A flight of stairs offers a wonderful opportunity for creating a warm and colorful welcome with cascades of flowers and foliage tumbling from containers. This planting takes advantage of the height of the stairs, with an abundance of plants trailing over the sides of the steps. The blue and gold scheme alternates the low-growing ageratum and lantana with the taller cornflowers and dahlias.

YOU WILL NEED

(quantities for two containers)
1 *Dahlia* 'Yellow Hammer' × 1, p.131
2 *Centaurea cyanus* 'Dwarf Blue' (cornflower) × 2, p.130
3 *Glechoma hederacea* 'Variegata' (variegated ground ivy) × 1, p.133
4 *Lysimachia nummularia* 'Aurea' × 1, p.135
5 *Lantana* 'Aloha' × 2, p.134
6 *Ageratum* 'Blue Danube' × 2, p.128

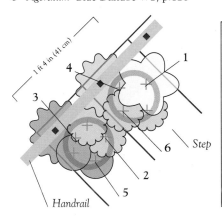

1 ft 4 in (41 cm)

Step

Handrail

ALTERNATIVE ARRANGEMENT

A simple but attractive alternative to a mixed planting is to feature two species, such as the geraniums and shade-loving impatiens used here, in varying tones of similar colors. In this display, the colors of the flowers range from white, through pale and dark pink, to vibrant red. On stairs that lead down below ground level, place plants with the palest flowers at the bottom of the steps to lighten the shady area, and position plants with the brightest flowers at the top.

Pelargonium 'Paintbox'

Impatiens 'Tempo Burgundy'

Pelargonium 'Tiffany'

Impatiens 'Accent Pink'

Pelargonium 'Cassandra'

Impatiens 'Accent White'

PLANTING SAFELY ON A FLIGHT OF STAIRS

A flight of stairs is a perfect location for displaying plants in containers, enabling you to achieve many different visual effects. Before deciding on an arrangement, assess the site. Consider the width and depth of each step, and make sure that the containers and their plants do not restrict your use of the stairs.

Galvanized florists' buckets (with drainage holes drilled in the bottom) have a modern feel and, since they are tall and slender, take up little space. Where possible, secure each container to a railing to avoid knocking it over. Wrap a piece of garden wire around each container, then tie it to the railing.

Dahlia
'Yellow Hammer'
*Tubers can be lifted, then
replanted in spring*

Ageratum
'Blue Danube'
*Tufts of flowers add
texture to display*

Centaurea cyanus
'Dwarf Blue'
*Long-lasting
cornflowers are
ideal for cutting*

MAINTAINING THE DISPLAY

Keep the plants well watered and fed
in summer, and deadhead flowers
regularly for a continuous show until
early autumn. Lantana will survive
winter indoors, so repot these plants
at this time. Lysimachia dies back in
winter to reappear in spring, while
ground ivy is often evergreen. Plant
Viola × wittrockiana and dwarf bulbs
for a winter and spring display.

Lantana 'Aloha'
*Flower clusters stand out
against dark green leaves*

Glechoma hederacea
'Variegata'
*Long stems can be trimmed to
encourage dense growth*

Lysimachia
nummularia 'Aurea'
*Fast-growing stems
will trail down steps*

YEAR-ROUND PLANTING

A small, shady space such as a recessed entrance can be transformed by an arrangement of plants that guarantee a continuous display in all but the coldest regions. Here, *Pyracantha* 'Teton' has delicate, evergreen leaves, white flowers in spring, and bright orange berries in autumn and winter, while *Hydrangea macrophylla* provides a late-summer burst of white blooms. Shiny-leaved *Fatsia japonica* and variegated *Euonymus fortunei* 'Gold Tip' are attractive in all seasons.

YOU WILL NEED

1 *Fatsia japonica* (Japanese aralia) × 1, p.132
2 *Euonymus fortunei* 'Gold Tip' × 1, p.132
3 *Hydrangea macrophylla* 'White Wave' × 1, p.134
4 *Pyracantha* 'Teton' (firethorn) × 1, p.137

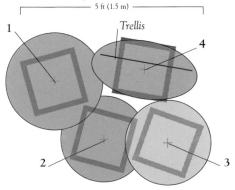

5 ft (1.5 m)

Trellis

1
4
2
3

Fatsia japonica
Foliage should be regularly cleaned with damp cloth (see p. 119)

Glossy leaves of fatsia are strikingly architectural and valuable in shade, since they reflect light

Fatsia will produce small, white flowers in autumn and black fruits in early winter

MAINTAINING THE DISPLAY

Pyracantha trained on a bamboo frame is ideal for standing against a wall. In spring, remove outward-growing shoots carefully, avoiding the long thorns. The hydrangea's leaves fall in winter, and its flowerheads fade to russet brown; if left, these will provide interest until cut when new growth appears.

Euonymus fortunei 'Gold Tip'
Variegation on young leaves is yellow, becoming cream with age

Pyracantha 'Teton'
In a sheltered, bird-free area, orange berries should last well into winter

Hydrangea macrophylla 'White Wave'
Acidic soil mix is used here and flowers remain pure white; in alkaline soil mix they are tinged pink

Limed wooden boxes bring welcome light to shady area (see p. 105)

FLIGHT OF STAIRS

Growing climbers around a handrail is an attractive way of brightening up a flight of stairs. Here, a waterproofed wooden box spans two steps to provide a sufficient depth of soil mix for the climbers. The ornamental purple grape *Vitis vinifera* 'Purpurea' gives the first hint of the planting's color scheme, which is continued with the wine-red of *Clematis* 'Vino', *Gaillardia pulchella* 'Red Plume', and *Imperata cylindrica* 'Rubra'.

YOU WILL NEED

1   *Imperata cylindrica* 'Rubra' (Japanese blood grass) × 3, p.134
2   *Clematis* 'Vino' × 1, p.131
3   *Gaillardia pulchella* 'Red Plume' (blanket flower) × 4, p.133
4   *Plectranthus forsteri* 'Marginatus' × 2, p.137
5   *Vitis vinifera* 'Purpurea' (purple-leaved grape) × 1, p.139

A STEP-SPANNING BOX

Use suitably treated lumber such as marine plywood to construct this box. Hardwoods such as teak can be used, but should come from a renewable source. Measure the height and depth of two steps, and have the wood cut so that the box will be a snug fit. When constructing the box, use two metal brackets to secure each joint, and drill drainage holes in the base (see p. 104). The exterior has been treated with waterproof varnish (see p. 105), but could be decorated with tiles or a paint finish instead.

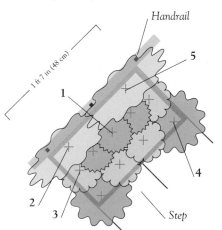

Handrail

1 ft 7 in (48 cm)

5

1

4

2

3

Step

VARIATION ON A THEME

This arrangement has a long season of interest. In late spring, the clematis bears its first flush of large, wine-red flowers, and the grape leaves are a mix of purple and green. These are complemented by the spring-flowering *Allium karataviense*, which produces drumstick-like, purple blooms. These bulbs should be planted in autumn.

Vitis vinifera 'Purpurea'

Clematis 'Vino'

Allium karataviense

Imperata cylindrica 'Rubra'

Plectranthus forsteri 'Marginatus'

MAINTAINING THE DISPLAY

Prune the clematis in early spring, removing old and weak growth, and trim the remaining shoots down to a pair of healthy buds. Tie in the young growths of the grape while they are green and supple, since they will become woody and stiff as they mature. The grape will respond well to cutting back once it spans the length of the handrail.

Vitis vinifera 'Purpurea'
Young, green foliage turns wine-red in summer and rich purple in autumn

Clematis 'Vino'
Tendrils cling to railings without extra support

Imperata cylindrica 'Rubra'
Thin streaks of red direct eye to center of arrangement

Gaillardia pulchella 'Red Plume'
Regular deadheading will ensure continuous flowering

Plectranthus forsteri 'Marginatus'
Trailing, variegated foliage is ideal for softening box edges

SHADY FERNS

Ferns thrive in shady conditions, making them ideal for livening up a wall that is rarely touched by sunlight. Ferns are available in many textures and forms, the pattern of their fronds varying from the delicate teardrops of *Adiantum raddianum* to the chunky stag's horns of *Platycerium bifurcatum*, so it is hard to believe that they belong to the same family. For a decorative background, paint the lines of the trellis in different colors.

MAINTAINING THE DISPLAY

Since ferns are woodland plants, most prefer rich, moist soil. Use a moisture-retentive, soil-based potting mix, enriched with leaf mold if possible, and make sure that it never becomes waterlogged or dries out. Feed with liquid fertilizer every two weeks in summer. The staghorn and bird's-nest ferns are not hardy and will need to be brought indoors in late summer, well before the first frost.

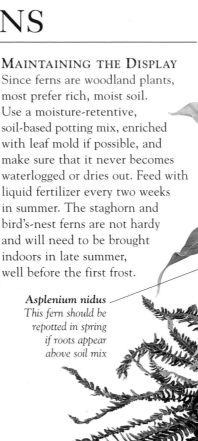

Asplenium nidus
This fern should be repotted in spring if roots appear above soil mix

Blechnum spicant
Oldest fronds should be trimmed in late spring to allow new fronds to unfurl

Adiantum raddianum
This prefers acidic soil mix

Painted, plastic pots have been used to minimize weight

YOU WILL NEED

1 *Asplenium nidus* (bird's-nest fern) × 1, p.129
2 *Blechnum spicant* (hard fern) × 2, p.130
3 *Adiantum raddianum* (delta maidenhair fern) × 2, p.128
4 *Platycerium bifurcatum* (staghorn fern) × 1, p.137
5 *Asplenium scolopendrium* (hart's-tongue fern) × 1, p.129

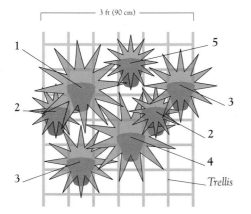

3 ft (90 cm)

Trellis

**Asplenium
scolopendrium**
*Shiny fronds unfurl
from center of plant*

*Ferns can be kept moist
in hot weather by using a
spray bottle to create fine
mist around them – avoid
directly spraying fronds*

**Platycerium
bifurcatum**
*Fronds are
covered with fine,
velvety coating*

BASKET OF PASTEL PINKS

Rosa 'Jeanne Lajoie', with its trailing habit and repeated flowering, is a miniature climbing rose that can be planted to make a superb hanging-basket display. Its pale pink flowers are complemented by the stronger pink of *Verbena* 'Pink Parfait' and the trailing lilac of *Lobelia pendula* 'Lilac Fountain' and *Convolvulus sabatius*. Plant the rose in a large basket to provide its roots with enough soil mix.

YOU WILL NEED

1 *Rosa* 'Jeanne Lajoie' (rose) × 1, p.138
2 *Convolvulus sabatius* syn. *C. mauritanicus* × 5, p.131
3 *Lobelia pendula* 'Lilac Fountain' × 5, p.135
4 *Verbena* 'Pink Parfait' × 5, p.139

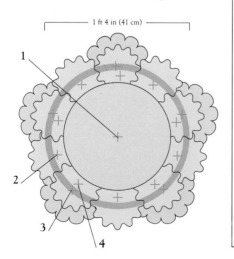

1 ft 4 in (41 cm)

MAINTAINING THE DISPLAY

Encourage bushy new growth on the lobelia by trimming it with scissors when it becomes straggly (see p. 121). For a continuous display of flowers, regularly deadhead the rose – cutting off each cluster of spent flowers – and the convolvulus. The rose can remain in the hanging basket for two seasons, but remove and replace the top few inches of soil mix before the plant starts into growth each spring. At the same time, prune some of the long branches back to an outward-facing bud. After two years, repot the rose, or plant it out.

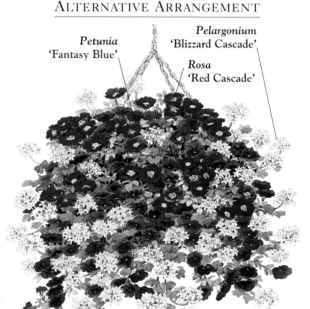

ALTERNATIVE ARRANGEMENT

Petunia 'Fantasy Blue'

Pelargonium 'Blizzard Cascade'

Rosa 'Red Cascade'

A red, white, and blue color scheme is particularly popular for a summer hanging basket, and there is a vast range of plants that can be used to make up this traditional combination. The display shown here features the deep red *Rosa* 'Red Cascade' as the focus of the arrangement and is filled out with the trailing, rich blue *Petunia* 'Fantasy Blue' and white *Pelargonium* 'Blizzard Cascade'.

Hanging basket should be watered at least once daily – twice daily if temperatures rise above 68°F (20°C)

Verbena 'Pink Parfait'
Petals range from pale to strong pink

Rosa
'Jeanne Lajoie'
Rose spreads to create blanket of color

Cutting back rose will encourage new, flowering shoots

Lobelia pendula
'Lilac Fountain'
Profusion of flowers soon fills gaps in arrangement

Convolvulus sabatius
Small, china-blue flowers are produced on long, trailing stems

GEOMETRIC TRILOGY

This arrangement relies on contrasting geometric shapes for its impact, which is reinforced by the clean lines of the plain terracotta containers. Scale is important here, too. The clipped globe of *Buxus sempervirens* bridges the difference in height between the pyramid of trained *Hedera canariensis* 'Gloire de Marengo' and the disk of low-growing *Impatiens* 'Super Elfin Red', enabling the eye to move comfortably from one shape to another.

MAINTAINING THE DISPLAY

These plants thrive in shade, and the evergreen ivy and boxwood will provide interest all year. In cold climates, impatiens will not survive the first frosts. Consider replacing them in autumn with a single-color, massed planting of winter-flowering *Viola* × *wittrockiana* (pansies) or shade-loving primroses.

New growth is tied in to frame with soft twine rather than woven through to allow for easy pruning (see p. 121)

Hedera canariensis 'Gloire de Marengo'
Large-leaved, cream-variegated ivy covers wooden frame quickly

Wooden topiary frame has been treated with coat of dark green woodstain

YOU WILL NEED

1 *Hedera canariensis* 'Gloire de Marengo' (Canary Island ivy) × 1, p.133
2 *Buxus sempervirens* (boxwood) × 1, p.130
3 *Impatiens* 'Super Elfin Red' (impatiens) × 7, p.134

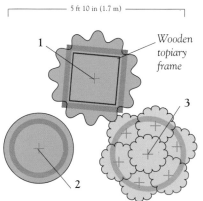

5 ft 10 in (1.7 m)

Wooden topiary frame

1

2

3

Buxus sempervirens
Boxwood is slow-growing but provides strong outline when final shape is achieved

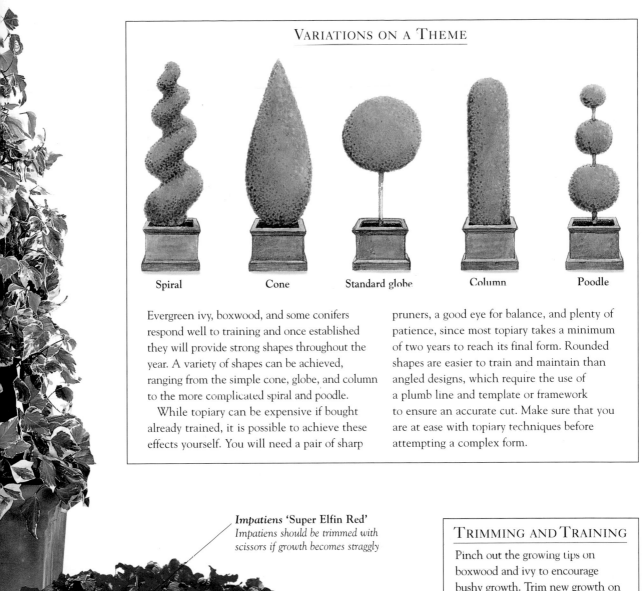

VARIATIONS ON A THEME

Spiral   Cone   Standard globe   Column   Poodle

Evergreen ivy, boxwood, and some conifers respond well to training and once established they will provide strong shapes throughout the year. A variety of shapes can be achieved, ranging from the simple cone, globe, and column to the more complicated spiral and poodle.

While topiary can be expensive if bought already trained, it is possible to achieve these effects yourself. You will need a pair of sharp pruners, a good eye for balance, and plenty of patience, since most topiary takes a minimum of two years to reach its final form. Rounded shapes are easier to train and maintain than angled designs, which require the use of a plumb line and template or framework to ensure an accurate cut. Make sure that you are at ease with topiary techniques before attempting a complex form.

Impatiens 'Super Elfin Red'
Impatiens should be trimmed with scissors if growth becomes straggly

Impatiens can be propagated by rooting cuttings in water (see p. 122)

TRIMMING AND TRAINING

Pinch out the growing tips on boxwood and ivy to encourage bushy growth. Trim new growth on the boxwood once or twice a year, during the growing season. Avoid cutting too much in one place (see p. 121). Keep the ivy trimmed when it has covered the frame. Always trim the stem just above a leaf, and avoid cutting the leaves themselves, since this will cause them to crinkle and turn brown. Occasionally remove one of the oldest shoots, and tie in new growth to fill the gap.

ORANGES & LEMONS

While most hanging baskets are filled with summer bedding plants, a small shrub can be just as successful. At the heart of this arrangement for a slightly shaded position is the dwarf shrub *Euonymus fortunei* 'Sunspot', with its trailing stems of dark green-and-gold leaves. It is accompanied by a mixed planting of begonias, lysimachias, nasturtiums, and mimulus in vibrant, eye-catching colors.

MAINTAINING THE DISPLAY

Euonymus fortunei is evergreen and, in all but the coldest regions, will provide interest in winter. Lysimachia dies back to grow again in spring and can be left in place all year. Lift the begonia tubers, and store them indoors in dry soil mix during winter. Introduce a splash of spring color by planting yellow crocus corms in autumn.

Lysimachia congestiflora **'Outback Sunset'**
Clusters of small, yellow flowers are surrounded by pale, variegated leaves

***Euonymus fortunei* 'Sunspot'**
After a few seasons, this shrub will outgrow its basket and should be replanted in a pot or garden

YOU WILL NEED

1 *Euonymus fortunei* 'Sunspot' × 1, p.132
2 *Begonia* × *tuberhybrida* 'Sensation Yellow' × 2, p.129
3 *Tropaeolum* 'Salmon Baby' (nasturtium) × 6, p.139
4 *Lysimachia congestiflora* 'Outback Sunset' × 4, p.135
5 *Mimulus* 'Viva' (monkeyflower) × 7, p.135

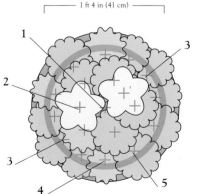

1 ft 4 in (41 cm)

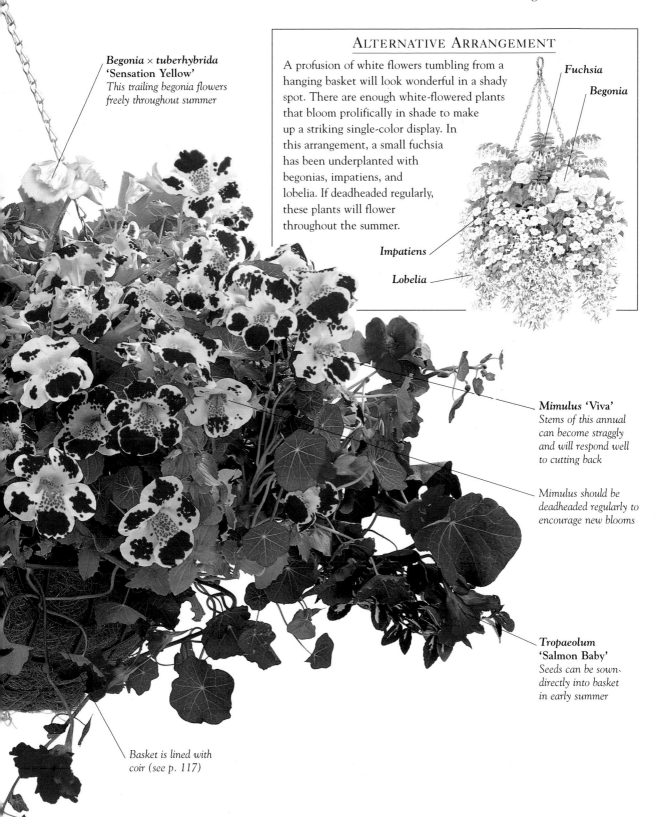

Begonia × *tuberhybrida*
'Sensation Yellow'
*This trailing begonia flowers
freely throughout summer*

ALTERNATIVE ARRANGEMENT

A profusion of white flowers tumbling from a
hanging basket will look wonderful in a shady
spot. There are enough white-flowered plants
that bloom prolifically in shade to make
up a striking single-color display. In
this arrangement, a small fuchsia
has been underplanted with
begonias, impatiens, and
lobelia. If deadheaded regularly,
these plants will flower
throughout the summer.

Fuchsia

Begonia

Impatiens

Lobelia

Mimulus 'Viva'
*Stems of this annual
can become straggly
and will respond well
to cutting back*

*Mimulus should be
deadheaded regularly to
encourage new blooms*

**Tropaeolum
'Salmon Baby'**
*Seeds can be sown
directly into basket
in early summer*

*Basket is lined with
coir (see p. 117)*

SMALL SPACES

BREEZY ROOFTOP
This arrangement makes ingenious
use of all available vertical space
to create a wall of living color in
a restricted rooftop area.

With a little imagination, it is possible to grow
plants in the smallest of places – whether on a
roof or by an entrance, on a balcony or a patio, or even
a deck – and there is enormous satisfaction to be gained
from creating a green haven in an unlikely site. If floor
space is limited, a wall can be adapted into a planting area.
These opportunities can be maximized by using plants
that are evergreen or have a long flowering season.

CREATIVE CORNER
A variety of plants, from aspidistras
to tree ferns, combined with natural
materials make this corner an ideal
transition between house and garden.

BARREL OF PINK

The compact growth and dense flowering of polyantha roses make them ideal for use in containers. The centerpiece for this arrangement, *Rosa* 'China Doll', produces a mass of flowers, ranging from pearly white to soft, shell-pink. Tones of mauve appear in the other pink blooms, from the large-flowered *Impatiens* New Guinea Hybrid to the delicate diascias.

YOU WILL NEED

1 *Rosa* 'China Doll' (rose)
   × 1, p.138
2 *Nemesia* 'Joan Wilder' × 1, p.136
3 *Diascia rigescens* × 1, p.131
4 *Helichrysum petiolare* × 3, p.133
5 *Impatiens* New Guinea Hybrid
   (impaties) × 4 planted in
   semi-circle, p.134
6 *Lobelia pendula* 'Lilac Fountain'
   × 3 planted in semi-circle, p.135
7 *Diascia vigilis* 'Elliott's Variety'
   × 1, p.131

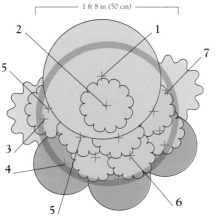

— 1 ft 8 in (50 cm) —

Rosa 'China Doll'
Clusters of flowers should be removed when most of blooms have faded

Nemesia 'Joan Wilder'
Tiny, yellow eye shines out from center of flower

Diascia rigescens
Cherry-pink flowers and trailing habit contrast with soft pink blooms and upright stems of 'Elliott's Variety'

**Diascia vigilis
'Elliott's Variety'**
*Spikes produce flowers
throughout summer*

**Impatiens New
Guinea Hybrid**
*This variety has larger
flowers and leaves than
other types of impatiens*

VARIATION ON A THEME

**Rosa 'Flower
Carpet'**

For a vibrant version of this arrangement, replace
Rosa 'China Doll' with the rose 'Flower Carpet'.
This variety produces vivid, cerise-pink flowers
in great numbers through the summer, and it
has been bred to withstand all the principal
diseases to which roses are susceptible.

Lobelia pendula 'Lilac Fountain'
*Deadheading will encourage fresh
growth (see p. 121)*

Helichrysum petiolare
*Silvery, trailing
foliage softens display*

*If helichrysum becomes
too vigorous, it can be
pruned back to new,
outward-facing side shoots*

MAINTAINING THE DISPLAY
Polyantha roses are easy to look after, since they are bred to stay
small and do not require complicated pruning. Once a flower
cluster has faded, trim it back to just above the first, outward-
facing leaf. At the point where the leaf joins the stem, a bud
will produce new flower-bearing shoots. To encourage flowering
on the accompanying plants, cut back fading spikes on the
diascias and nemesias, and pinch out dying impatiens blooms.

*Smoky blue stain
applied to oak half-
barrel sets off pink
tones to perfection*

BASKETS OF FLOWERS

The weight and texture of wicker baskets make them perfect for use as containers. Here, the color of the baskets is reflected in the planting. The stems of the *Aralia elata* 'Variegata', the petals of the *Verbena* 'Peaches and Cream', and the backs of the *Nicotiana* 'Havana Appleblossom' flowers all have the same peachy-tan tone. White flowers add contrast, and herbs are included for their attractive leaves.

YOU WILL NEED

1   *Verbena* 'White Kleopatra' × 3, p.139
2   *Petunia* 'Junior Fantasy White' × 3, p.137
3   *Ageratum* 'Summer Snow' × 2, p.128
4   *Petroselinum crispum* var. *neapolitanum* (flat-leaved parsley) × 4, p.136
5   *Verbena* 'Peaches and Cream' × 3, p.139
6   *Anethum graveolens* (dill) × 4, p.129
7   *Nicotiana* 'Havana Appleblossom' (flowering tobacco) × 4, p.136
8   *Aralia elata* 'Variegata' (Japanese angelica tree) × 1, p.129

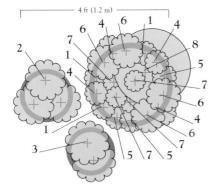

Anethum graveolens
Yellow flowers can be pinched out to encourage leaf growth

Aralia elata 'Variegata'
Shoots whose leaves revert to plain green should be removed

Verbena 'White Kleopatra'
This variety produces dense spheres of white flowers

MAINTAINING THE DISPLAY

Aralia is a stunning, architectural shrub and is ideal for use in a container in a sunny position – it will even tolerate a little shade. This variegated form is not as hardy as the plain green variety and will benefit from protection in winter. In summer, deadhead nicotianas, verbenas, ageratums, and petunias regularly to ensure continuous flowering. Add spring interest to the small baskets by planting bulbs such as crocus or scillas.

Petunia 'Junior Fantasy White'
Cream at center of trumpet fades to ivory white at edge of petals

Ageratum 'Summer Snow'
Clusters of feathery flowers bring unusual texture to arrangement

VARIATION ON A THEME

Petunia 'Blue Vein'

Petunia 'Purple Wave'

Verbena 'Carousel'

Impatiens

Helichrysum petiolare

A treated wicker shopping basket (see p. 117) makes a perfect hanging basket. Here, trailing varieties of some of the plants featured in the main arrangement tumble attractively from the container. The cascading stems of *Petunia* 'Purple Wave' and *P.* 'Blue Vein' are complemented by a planting of the striped flowers of *Verbena* 'Carousel'. Double impatiens add height to the center, while helichrysum trails over the edge.

Nicotiana 'Havana Appleblossom'
Star-shaped flowers brighten center of display

Petroselinum crispum var. neapolitanum
This parsley can be used for cooking

Basket is lined with black plastic (see p. 117)

Verbena 'Peaches and Cream'
Flowerheads combine shades of salmon and coral pink with a hint of yellow

TREATING WICKER

When selecting a basket to use as a container, choose a stout, wicker type that will last for the longest possible time. Consider your planting design before deciding on the finish for the basket. To retain the natural color of wicker, use clear, matte varnish for weatherproofing. Alternatively, achieve an attractive effect by treating the wicker with colored woodstains in shades such as jade green, duck-egg blue, or warm, rusty red. Make sure that the color will blend with the planting design that you have in mind.

BLACK & WHITE CONTRAST

There are few plants with black or deep purple flowers, and fewer still with black leaves. Contrasted with white, they look very striking and, planted in a galvanized metal container, make a distinctly contemporary arrangement. *Ophiopogon planiscapus* is black through the year, while the green-and-white variegated grass, *Holcus mollis*, is at its whitest when new growth appears in spring.

YOU WILL NEED

1 *Tulipa* 'Queen of Night' (tulip) × 6 planted randomly, p.139
2 *Ophiopogon planiscapus* 'Nigrescens' × 6, p.136
3 *Holcus mollis* 'Albovariegatus' (variegated creeping soft grass) × 6, p.134
4 *Tulipa* 'Maureen' (tulip) × 13 planted randomly, p.139
5 *Muscari botryoides* 'Album' (grape hyacinth) × 12, p.135

Holcus mollis **'Albovariegatus'** *In early spring, new, bright, white foliage can be encouraged by trimming plant back to 4 in (10 cm) in height*

1 ft 8 in (50 cm)

Tulipa 'Queen of Night'
This tulip produces single flowers in late spring

Tulipa 'Maureen'
Ivory-white petals highlighted by wide, green leaves

Muscari botryoides 'Album'
Flower spikes will last for up to three weeks

Ophiopogon planiscapus 'Nigrescens'
In summer, small lilac flowers can be removed to preserve black-and-white theme

VARIATION ON A THEME

Cosmos sulphureus 'Ladybird Scarlet'

Viola 'Bowles' Black'

Viola cornuta alba

Continue the black-and-white theme into the summer by replacing the tulips with long-flowering violas such as *Viola* 'Bowles' Black' and *Viola cornuta alba*. A stark contrast can be created by adding scarlet to the arrangement with *Cosmos sulphureus* 'Ladybird Scarlet'.

Complete display

Base of container is drilled with drainage holes (see p. 105)

MAINTAINING THE DISPLAY
This spring arrangement is ideally suited to a sunny position. Remove the tulips after flowering to avoid unsightly dying foliage. Keep the muscaris in the container and, as the leaves die, provide a liquid feed to ensure free flowering the following year.

DRAMATIC OUTLINES

A celebration of contrasting, architectural foliage, this group will look impressive against a white wall where the spiky leaves and their shadows will form striking patterns. Although *Acanthus mollis* produces bold spires of purple and white flowers in summer, it has been included here for its solid, glossy leaves. Their curvaceous shapes are an effective contrast to the narrow, sword-like foliage of the cordyline and yucca.

MAINTAINING THE DISPLAY

Despite their exotic appearances, most of these plants will tolerate short periods of cold and, in warmer regions, the acanthus will keep its leaves throughout the winter in a sheltered site. The bamboo is rather hardy, but the yucca, chamaerops, and cordyline will need to be brought indoors during the coldest months of the year.

YOU WILL NEED

1 *Chamaerops humilis* (dwarf fan palm) × 1, p.130
2 *Cordyline australis* 'Torbay Dazzler' (New Zealand cabbage palm) × 1, p.131
3 *Acanthus mollis* (bear's breeches) × 1, p.128
4 *Yucca filamentosa* (adam's needle) × 1, p.139
5 *Fargesia murieliae* 'Simba' (bamboo) × 1, p.132

Chamaerops humilis
Dead fronds should be cut away at base with a sharp knife, flush with stem

Chamaerops may produce tiny, yellow flowers in summer

Angular, terracotta container complements straight lines of wooden decking

Coarse sand added to soil-based mix ensures free drainage

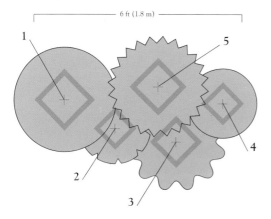

— 6 ft (1.8 m) —

Fargesia murieliae 'Simba'
*In spring, some old canes of this
bamboo can be pruned at base
to encourage fresh, new growth*

Acanthus mollis
*After flowering, flower
spike should be cut out to
enable plant to produce new
leaves, rather than set seed*

Yucca filamentosa
*Deep green leaves are
edged with white threads*

Cordyline australis 'Torbay Dazzler'
*Old leaves should be removed
as their variegation fades*

*Evergreen leaves should be
wiped with a damp cloth to
keep them clean (see p. 119)*

SPRING BALANCE

A shrub such as a *Viburnum tinus*, trained as a topiary, is an ideal substitute for a tree in a container, adding permanent structure to an arrangement. The evergreen viburnum changes with the seasons – red buds in winter open into blush-white flowers in spring. Here, an underplanting of *Tulipa* 'Angelique' reflects the pink tinge of the shrub's flowers. The topiary and planter are perfectly balanced in size and style, while the ivy softens the edges of the container.

YOU WILL NEED

1 *Hedera helix* 'Esther' (ivy) × 4, p.133
2 *Tulipa* 'Angelique' (tulip) × 12, p.139
3 Standard (topiary) *Viburnum tinus* × 1, p.139

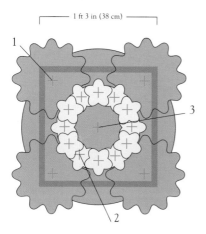

| 1 ft 3 in (38 cm) |

VARIATIONS ON A THEME

SUMMER DECORATION
Once the tulips have finished flowering, you can replace them with shade-tolerant, tuberous begonias. Try the highly decorative, double varieties, such as B. × *tuberhybrida* 'Non-stop', and smaller flowered, trailing types, such as B. *pendula* 'Illumination'. Fuchsias or impatiens would look equally good.

Begonia × *tuberhybrida* 'Non-stop'

Begonia pendula 'Illumination'

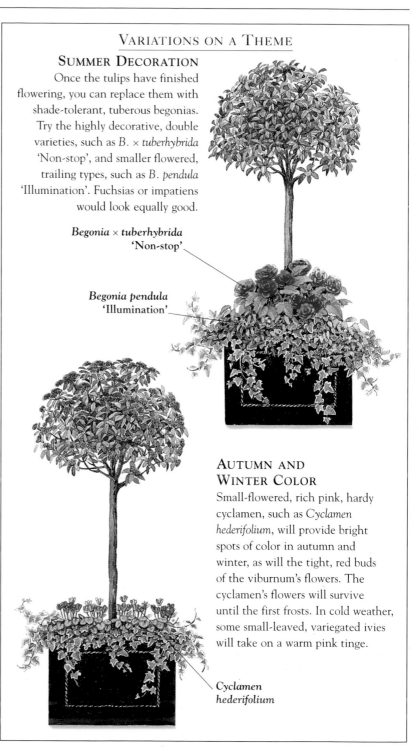

AUTUMN AND WINTER COLOR
Small-flowered, rich pink, hardy cyclamen, such as *Cyclamen hederifolium*, will provide bright spots of color in autumn and winter, as will the tight, red buds of the viburnum's flowers. The cyclamen's flowers will survive until the first frosts. In cold weather, some small-leaved, variegated ivies will take on a warm pink tinge.

Cyclamen hederifolium

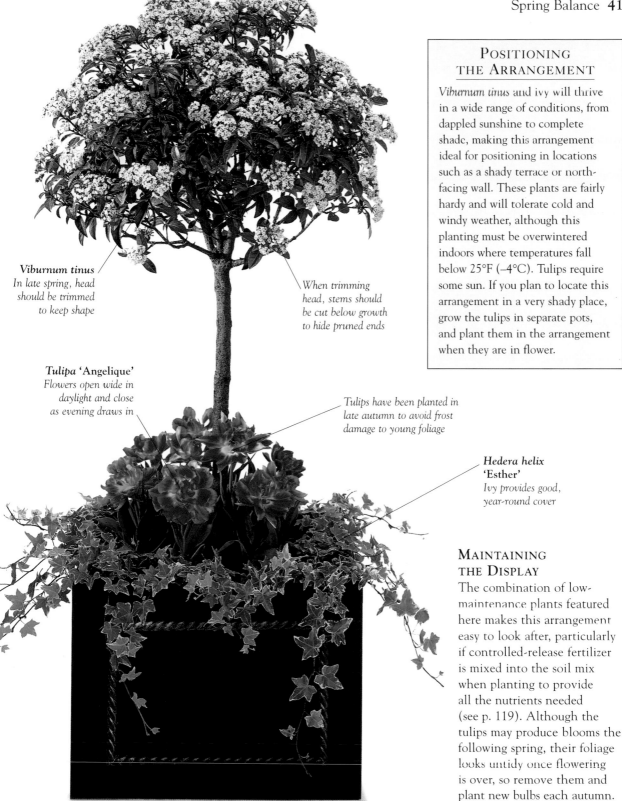

Viburnum tinus
*In late spring, head
should be trimmed
to keep shape*

*When trimming
head, stems should
be cut below growth
to hide pruned ends*

Tulipa 'Angelique'
*Flowers open wide in
daylight and close
as evening draws in*

*Tulips have been planted in
late autumn to avoid frost
damage to young foliage*

**Hedera helix
'Esther'**
*Ivy provides good,
year-round cover*

POSITIONING THE ARRANGEMENT

Viburnum tinus and ivy will thrive in a wide range of conditions, from dappled sunshine to complete shade, making this arrangement ideal for positioning in locations such as a shady terrace or north-facing wall. These plants are fairly hardy and will tolerate cold and windy weather, although this planting must be overwintered indoors where temperatures fall below 25°F (–4°C). Tulips require some sun. If you plan to locate this arrangement in a very shady place, grow the tulips in separate pots, and plant them in the arrangement when they are in flower.

MAINTAINING THE DISPLAY

The combination of low-maintenance plants featured here makes this arrangement easy to look after, particularly if controlled-release fertilizer is mixed into the soil mix when planting to provide all the nutrients needed (see p. 119). Although the tulips may produce blooms the following spring, their foliage looks untidy once flowering is over, so remove them and plant new bulbs each autumn.

RUST & CREAM TRIANGLES

Triangular containers are
unusual but extremely versatile,
since they can be arranged
in a number of different
configurations. The bold,
architectural forms of these
boxes call for equally bold
plantings. The sword-like leaves
of Phormium tenax 'Bronze
Baby' are echoed by those of
Crocosmia 'Emily McKenzie'
and the red-hot pokers. Cool
Helichrysum petiolare takes the
heat out of the display and
softens the edges of the boxes.

MAINTAINING THE DISPLAY

Position this arrangement in a sunny site, and ensure that the
soil mix is well drained. Cut fading red-hot poker spikes at their
bases to ensure continuous flowering. Crocosmia tubers can be
left in place over winter, or removed and stored in dry sand or
soil mix. Keep the red-hot pokers in place throughout winter,
but protect their crowns (see p. 109). In spring, remove any
damaged leaves from the evergreen phormiums and helichrysums.

Kniphofia 'Little Maid'
*This dwarf variety reaches
a maximum height of
2 ft (60 cm)*

Kniphofia uvaria
*Flowers attract
butterflies and bees*

YOU WILL NEED

1 Crocosmia 'Emily McKenzie'
× 9, p.131
2 Kniphofia uvaria (red-hot poker)
× 4, p.134
3 Kniphofia 'Little Maid' (red-hot
poker) × 3, p.134
4 Helichrysum petiolare × 6, p.133
5 Phormium tenax 'Bronze Baby'
(New Zealand flax) × 2, p.137

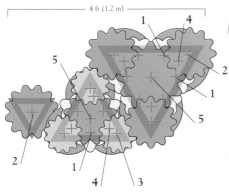

*Warm brown of
wood complements
colors of planting*

***Phormium tenax
'Bronze Baby'***
*Narrow leaves are evergreen,
providing interest all year*

*Bronze phormium
foliage reinforces
fiery theme*

***Crocosmia
'Emily
McKenzie'***
*Bright orange,
star-like flowers
with darker,
burnt orange
throats will
appear in
late summer*

***Helichrysum
petiolare***
*This foliage plant
will keep its leaves
during mild winters*

COPPER CONTRASTS

The informal planting of a combination of perennials and grasses works as well in containers as it does in borders. Here, the copper tone of the water cylinder made the choice of *Carex comans* 'Bronze Form' and *Acaena microphylla* 'Kupferteppich' an obvious one, while the open, airy habits of *Verbena bonariensis* and *Miscanthus sinensis* balance the solid, cylindrical mass of the container perfectly.

YOU WILL NEED

1 *Acaena microphylla* 'Kupferteppich'
  × 4, p.128
2 *Verbena bonariensis* syn. *V. patagonica*
  × 3, p.139
3 *Carex comans* 'Bronze Form'
  × 2, p.130
4 *Miscanthus sinensis* 'Morning Light'
  × 1, p.135

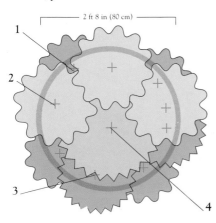

2 ft 8 in (80 cm)

SUNNY SEDGE
Carex comans 'Bronze Form' has an attractive, weeping habit and delicate, rust-colored flowers. Its warm bronze foliage is striking when lit by the sun. Take this into consideration when positioning the plant.

Arching foliage is quite hardy

VARIATION ON A THEME

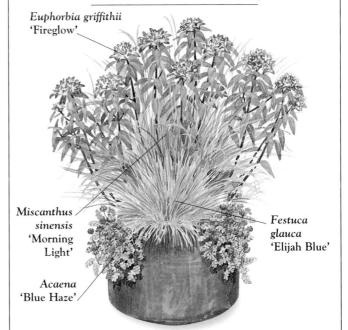

Euphorbia griffithii 'Fireglow'

Miscanthus sinensis 'Morning Light'

Acaena 'Blue Haze'

Festuca glauca 'Elijah Blue'

Continuing the metallic theme, this version of the arrangement keeps the miscanthus in position and replaces *Acaena microphylla* 'Kupferteppich' with steel-gray A. 'Blue Haze', which produces russet flowers in summer. The carex has been replaced by silver-blue *Festuca glauca* 'Elijah Blue', while copper-orange flowered *Euphorbia griffithii* 'Fireglow' takes the place of the verbena.

Verbena bonariensis
*Flowers are attractive
to butterflies*

**Miscanthus sinensis
'Morning Light'**
*This grass produces
tall, fluffy, white
seedheads in autumn*

**Carex comans
'Bronze Form'**
*Rust-colored foliage
curls over edge of cylinder*

**Acaena microphylla
'Kupferteppich'**
*This should be trimmed with
scissors if it becomes too vigorous*

MAINTAINING THE DISPLAY
In winter the dead stems of *Verbena
bonariensis* have an attractive, architectural
appearance. Leave the stems in place until
early spring, then cut them back to the
base of the plant. The foliage of *Miscanthus
sinensis* fades to a pleasing, pale biscuit
color in autumn as it dies back. Enjoy
its winter display, then cut it back in
early spring. *Acaena microphylla* and
Carex comans are both evergreen.

*Weathered
copper will
develop green
patina*

TOWERS OF SUCCULENTS

Fleshy succulents have wonderfully complex, architectural shapes. This arrangement includes the needle-sharp spikes of *Agave americana*, the rosettes of *Echeveria* and purple-brown *Aeonium arboreum* 'Zwartkop', and the thick, textured tails of *Sedum morganianum*. These are best displayed in simple containers with clean, angular lines. Here, a clay pipe and chimney liners from a builder's supply have been used. A single piece of driftwood adds to the sculptural feel of the display.

YOU WILL NEED

1 *Echeveria elegans* × 3, p.132
2 *Aeonium arboreum* 'Zwartkop' (purple rose tree) × 1, p.128
3 *Sedum morganianum* (burro's tail) × 1, p.138
4 *Echeveria* hybrid × 3, p.132
5 *Agave americana* 'Variegata' (century plant) × 1, p.128

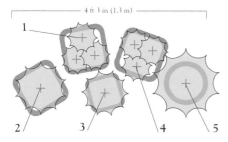

4 ft 3 in (1.3 m)

1

2   3   4   5

Aeonium arboreum 'Zwartkop'
Young leaves are green but become purple in sun

Echeveria elegans
Rosettes produce orange-pink flowers in summer

After flowering, stem should be trimmed back to base

MAINTAINING THE DISPLAY

Succulents require a frost-free climate if they are to remain outdoors all year. In cold areas, bring the plants indoors before the first frost. Succulents respond well to cool, sunny conditions, so position this collection in a room where the temperature is between 50–60°F (10–15°C) and where the plants will receive some direct sunlight during the day.

***Agave americana* 'Variegata'**
Agave should be handled with great care since its spines are very sharp

Echeveria hybrid
Main plant has produced offsets to form mass of rosettes

Agave planted in gritty, free-draining, soil-based mix

Plant is kept in container and slotted into chimney liner to allow easy removal

Sedum morganianum
Tails will continue to grow in length

Gnarled driftwood contrasts with smooth lines of clay pipes

SHADY COMPANIONS

One of the advantages of gardening in containers rather than in open ground is the possibility of growing plants side by side that require different soil conditions. *Camellia japonica* 'Alba Simplex' needs an acidic soil, while *Clematis campaniflora* prefers a more alkaline soil. Here, they are grown together in a double box, which provides each plant with its own ideal conditions. Their different flowering times ensure a long season of interest.

MAINTAINING THE DISPLAY

The key to successfully maintaining this arrangement is its location. Camellias and hostas thrive in dappled shade, but avoid an east-facing position, since the early sun may thaw the camellia's buds and flowers too quickly, causing them to turn brown. Ideally, the box should be positioned so that the camellia's leaves provide the shade needed for the roots of the clematis. Prune the clematis in early spring by cutting back the previous season's growth to the lowest pair of buds.

Camellia japonica 'Alba Simplex'
Dust should be removed from leaves to keep plant healthy (see p. 119)

YOU WILL NEED

1 *Camellia japonica* 'Alba Simplex' × 1, p.130
2 *Clematis campaniflora* × 1, p.130
3 *Argyranthemum frutescens* (marguerite) × 3, p.129
4 *Hosta undulata* var. *univittata* (plantain lily) × 4, p.134
5 *Blechnum spicant* (hard fern) × 1, p.130

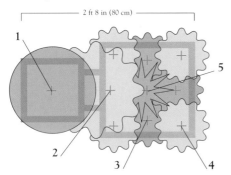

2 ft 8 in (80 cm)

VARIATION ON A THEME

Anemone blanda 'Atrocaerulea'

Prune the clematis in late winter to allow the camellia to display its flowers unimpeded in late spring. The group is enhanced by the addition of *Anemone blanda* 'Atrocaerulea', with its blue flowers circling the fern. As the camellia's blooms fade, the clematis will start to produce new growth.

Combination of acidic soil mix and fertilizer for acid-loving plant keeps foliage glossy, dark green

Clematis campaniflora
*Delicate, blue-tinged,
bell-like flowers dangle
from thin, twining stems*

Complete
display

*Boxes joined by
partition to allow
clematis to grow
through camellia*

Blechnum spicant
*This shade-loving, evergreen
fern is quite hardy*

**Argyranthemum
frutescens**
*Marguerites flower most
freely in sun but will give
a good show in shade*

**Hosta undulata
var. univittata**
*Slug and snail damage
can be avoided by using
a deterrent (see p. 77)*

*Box finished with
verdigris paint effect
(see p. 106) and
sealed with varnish*

HOT COLORS

Bright, hot colors such as scarlet, orange, and yellow can look wonderfully tropical in a sunny spot, particularly when positioned against a white wall. Here, the flowers of *Abutilon* 'Orangeade', *Eccremocarpus scaber*, and *Crocosmia* 'Lucifer' form a striking combination, and their leaves provide an interesting contrast. The tall, arching stems of *Phygelius capensis* and the trailing growth of *Bidens ferulifolia* create a strong shape, while the flowers of *Bracteantha bracteata* complete the bold arrangement.

MAINTAINING THE DISPLAY

This is a display for a frost-free site, although the eccremocarpus and phygelius are hardy to about 30°F (–1°C), with their top growth dying back and new shoots produced in spring. Remove old growth from the abutilon at this time. In summer, cut back any straggly stems on the bidens to form an attractive, bushy shape.

Phygelius capensis 'Indian Chief'
Coral-red, tubular flowers appear in summer months

Bidens ferulifolia
Daisy-like blooms are produced on trailing stems

Handmade terracotta tiles complement display

YOU WILL NEED

1. *Phygelius capensis* 'Indian Chief' × 1, p.137
2. *Bidens ferulifolia* × 3, p.130
3. *Bracteantha bracteata* 'Bright Bikini' (strawflower) × 3, p.130
4. *Abutilon* 'Orangeade' × 1, p.128
5. *Eccremocarpus scaber* (Chilean glory flower) × 1, p.132
6. *Crocosmia* 'Lucifer' × 5, p.131

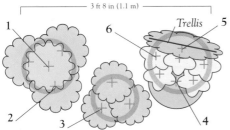

3 ft 8 in (1.1 m)

Trellis

Crocosmia 'Lucifer'
Flowers are produced in midsummer

Eccremocarpus scaber
Tendrils wrap themselves around trellis

Eccremocarpus can be raised from seed (see p. 123)

Bracteantha bracteata 'Bright Bikini'
Cut flowers can be dried by hanging in warm place

Abutilon 'Orangeade'
New growth can be encouraged by pruning old stems in spring

Warm ochre glazed pots allow brilliant colors of arrangement to take center stage

JAPANESE-STYLE GROUP

The elegant simplicity of a Japanese-style planting works well in a modern, urban setting, emphasized in this group by the use of galvanized trashcans as containers. The branches of *Corylus avellana* 'Contorta', bare in winter, resemble the minimal style of ikebana and are partnered here with an underplanting of moss-like *Soleirolia soleirolii*. The mat-forming *Bacopa* creates a horizontal line for the eye, and the spiky *Hakonechloa macra* 'Aureola', a vertical line.

YOU WILL NEED

1 *Bacopa* 'Snowflake' × 1, p.129
2 *Hakonechloa macra* 'Aureola' × 1, p.133
3 *Corylus avellana* 'Contorta' (contorted hazel) × 1, p.131
4 *Soleirolia soleirolii* (baby's tears) × 4, p.138

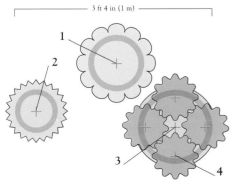

3 ft 4 in (1 m)

MAINTAINING THE DISPLAY

Contorted hazel is at its most interesting in winter and spring, when the leaves have fallen and pale gold catkins dangle from its bare stems. Since the glory of this shrub lies in its stark, twisted stems, use sharp pruners to prune out only dead, diseased, or damaged wood. In spring, as new growth pushes through, trim back the brown, winter leaves and flowerheads of *Hakonechloa*. Position *Bacopa* in a frost-free site for year-round growth. The baby's tears are not hardy and so must be kept in a frost-free site for the winter.

Bacopa 'Snowflake'
This spreads quickly to form a mat of fresh, green leaves and small, white flowers

Hakonechloa macra 'Aureola'
Golden spring and summer growth turns coppery brown when flowerheads and leaves die in autumn

Weathering reduces sheen on cans

Stones add finishing touch to Japanese style

Corylus avellana
'Contorta'
Long, pale catkins
appear on contorted
hazel in late winter, and
last throughout spring

Angular, twisted
branches give
architectural
interest to setting

Soleirolia soleirolii
This fast grower
quickly fills its
allotted space

Baby's tears can
be propagated
by division
(see p. 123)

(see p. 123)

ALTERNATIVE ARRANGEMENT

Pleioblastus
auricomus

Acer palmatum
var. dissectum

Juniperus
procumbens
'Nana'

When planning a Japanese-style group, it is important
to consider the geometric effect of the plants that you
are using. Here, *Pleioblastus auricomus* (bamboo) forms
vertical lines, while *Acer palmatum* var. *dissectum*
(Japanese maple) and *Juniperus procumbens* 'Nana' (Bonin
Island juniper) are predominantly horizontal. The range
of textures in the group's foliage adds to its impact.

SUNSHINE IN SHADE

Foliage can be as colorful as flowers and, if it is evergreen, will provide a year-round display. At the heart of this cheerful, golden arrangement for a shady spot is an evergreen, spiky *Mahonia japonica*, together with a brightly variegated *Euonymus fortunei*. *Epimedium × versicolor* and *Lysimachia nummularia* are featured here for their attractive foliage and delicate flowers, while *Nicotiana* 'Lime Green' is included for its fragrant flowers alone.

YOU WILL NEED

1 *Mahonia japonica* × 1, p.135
2 *Epimedium × versicolor* 'Sulphureum' × 4, p.132
3 *Lysimachia nummularia* 'Aurea' (creeping Jenny) × 4, p.135
4 *Euonymus fortunei* 'Emerald 'n' Gold' × 1, p.132
5 *Nicotiana* 'Lime Green' (flowering tobacco) × 4, p.136

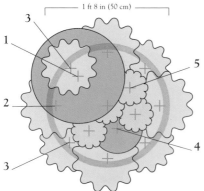

1 ft 8 in (50 cm)

Mahonia japonica
Mahonia grows slowly when its roots are confined; when it outgrows container it can be replaced with a small specimen

Euonymus fortunei 'Emerald 'n' Gold'
Low-growing shrub can be lightly trimmed to maintain size

Lysimachia nummularia 'Aurea'
Trailing stems produce yellow, buttercup-like flowers in summer

Purple-blue berries will appear on mahonia in spring

Nicotiana 'Lime Green'
Its flowers produce a light, pleasant scent at night

VARIATION ON A THEME

Choisya ternata 'Sundance'

Mahonia japonica

Lobelia pendula

Hedera helix 'Pittsburgh'

Vinca minor 'Variegata'

Mahonia japonica is a striking plant for a shady position. Alter the color scheme of the surrounding display by including plants with blue and white flowers. Mahonia is accompanied here by golden-leaved *Choisya ternata* 'Sundance', dark green ivy, the blue flowers of *Vinca minor* 'Variegata', and a mixture of *Lobelia pendula* cultivars.

Epimedium × versicolor 'Sulphureum'
Heart-shaped leaves have reddish purple tinge in spring

Galvanized tin tub is painted dark blue to heighten impact of golden plants

MAINTAINING THE DISPLAY

In addition to its attractive foliage, mahonia produces sprays of scented, yellow flowers from late autumn to spring. When the flowers have faded, remove them along with any discolored leaves. Trim old foliage from the epimediums and *Euonymus* in spring to encourage new growth. Creeping Jenny dies back in winter, and the nicotianas will need to be replaced each year. For late winter and spring interest, plant shade-tolerant, woodland bulbs such as *Erythronium* 'Pagoda' with its pale yellow, bell-like flowers.

BALCONY PLANTING

The success of a balcony display depends on it looking good from inside the room and from below. Here, *Hedera helix* 'Golden Ingot' forms a curtain of color down the back of the container. Through the railings climbs *Clematis flammula*, its flowers producing an almond fragrance that will be carried by the breeze. At the center of the display are apricot- and peach-colored flowers that create a warm glow all summer long.

View from street level

YOU WILL NEED

1   *Clematis flammula* × 1, p.130
2   *Hedera helix* 'Golden Ingot' (ivy)
    × 4, p.133
3   *Salvia coccinea* 'Coral Nymph'
    × 6, p.138
4   *Helichrysum petiolare* 'Aureum'
    × 3, p.133
5   *Verbena* 'Peaches and Cream' × 6, p.139
6   *Rosa* 'Sweet Magic' (rose) × 1, p.138
7   *Diascia* 'Blackthorn Apricot' × 4, p.131

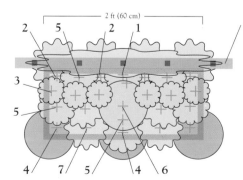

***Hedera helix*
'Golden Ingot'**
*Evergreen ivy is suitable
for windy conditions
above ground level*

***Diascia* 'Blackthorn Apricot'**
*Clusters of delicate flowers are
produced throughout summer*

***Helichrysum petiolare* 'Aureum'**
*Trailing foliage provides interest
at front of container*

MAINTAINING THE DISPLAY
Keep this balcony arrangement in good condition with timely pruning. To encourage new flower growth, trim spent flower clusters on the diascias and verbenas, and prune the stems of faded rose blooms back to the nearest outward-facing leaf. The golden helichrysum responds well to being cut back during the growing season. Remove ivy leaves that revert to plain green.

Clematis flammula
Dead growth on clematis should be trimmed back almost to base of plant in late winter

Salvia coccinea 'Coral Nymph'
Flower spikes produce shrimp-like blooms through summer

Rosa 'Sweet Magic'
This low-growing rose provides sturdy frame for delicate plants surrounding it

Rose will reach maximum height of 1½ ft (45 cm)

Verbena 'Peaches and Cream'
Leaves are prone to mildew if plant is not well watered

Container is treated with varnish to weatherproof and bring out grain

WINDOW-LEDGES

PROFUSION OF FLOWERS
The exuberant colors and vigorous
growth of these geraniums are
used effectively to create an
eye-catching balcony arrangement.

Almost any plant can be grown on a windowledge, from climbers and shrubs to herbs and cacti, provided it receives all the nutrients and water it needs. Attractive, well-planted windowboxes not only brighten up the façades of buildings for the benefit of passersby, but also offer an opportunity to frame the views from indoors with living color. A successful combination of containers and plants adds to the overall visual impact of an arrangement.

STRIKING SIMPLICITY
A simple, restrained planting of
geraniums, petunias, and lobelia is
displayed to perfection in an ornate,
weathered, terracotta windowbox.

GOLD & BLUE

The color combination of gold and blue is an attractive sight, always appearing fresh and yet warm. Here, the yellow-green foliage of *Helichrysum petiolare*, the variegated *Salvia officinalis*, and delicate *Felicia amelloides* create an impression of softness, with their matte textures and pale tones. The blue salvia, brachyscome, and felicia flowers stand out against this background, complemented by the handmade tiles on the box.

YOU WILL NEED

1 *Salvia farinacea* 'Victoria' × 6, p.138
2 *Euonymus fortunei* 'Emerald 'n' Gold' × 2, p.132
3 *Felicia amelloides* 'Variegata' (blue marguerite) × 2, p.132
4 *Salvia officinalis* 'Icterina' (golden sage) × 2, p.138
5 *Helichrysum petiolare* 'Aureum' × 1, p.133
6 *Brachyscome multifida* (Swan River daisy) × 2, p.130

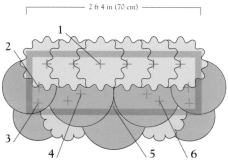

— 2 ft 4 in (70 cm) —

1
2
3
4 5 6

Brachyscome multifida
Brachyscome should be lightly trimmed to keep bushy habit

Salvia officinalis 'Icterina'
Sage leaves can be used for cooking

Salvia farinacea 'Victoria'
Tall flower spikes bloom from summer to autumn

VARIATION ON A THEME

Primula Pacific Series

Tulipa 'Showwinner'

For a startling spring display, combine vibrant scarlet with the gold foliage featured in the main arrangement. Plant dwarf tulip bulbs in autumn and add red *Primula* Pacific Series plants for the splashes of gold at the centers of their flowers.

Euonymus fortunei 'Emerald 'n' Gold'
Evergreen, variegated leaves remain bright green throughout winter

Felicia amelloides 'Variegata'
Yellow centers of felicia flowers complement gold foliage of display

Tiles have been laid on wooden window-box (see p. 107)

Helichrysum petiolare 'Aureum'
Velvety leaves trail over box

MAINTAINING THE DISPLAY

The framework of this arrangement can remain in place throughout the winter, since *Euonymus* is evergreen and *Salvia officinalis* and helichrysum will survive if kept in a sheltered, frost-free location. Replace the flowering plants – felicia, brachyscome, and *Salvia farinacea* – with blue pansies or primroses for winter color.

WARM PINK & WINE-RED

Free-flowering roses are ideal for containers, giving a display from midsummer through to the first frosts. Here, a harmonious effect is achieved by mixing the exquisite, pale pink flowers of *Rosa* 'Simplex' with tones that come from the same part of the color spectrum. The dwarf, wine-red barberry *Berberis thunbergii* 'Rose Glow' produces new foliage splashed with a similar shade of pink, and the annuals, *Verbena* 'Pink Kleopatra' and *Impatiens* New Guinea Hybrid, have flowers from the same tonal range.

YOU WILL NEED

1 *Rosa* 'Simplex' (rose) × 2, p.138
2 *Impatiens* New Guinea Hybrid (impatiens) × 5, p.134
3 *Verbena* 'Pink Kleopatra' × 4, p.139
4 *Berberis thunbergii* 'Rose Glow' (barberry) × 1, p.130

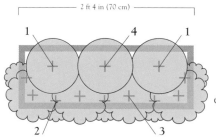

2 ft 4 in (70 cm)

Berberis thunbergii 'Rose Glow'
Barberry will produce small, yellow flowers in spring that can be pinched out to preserve color scheme

Verbena 'Pink Kleopatra'
Clusters of delicate pink flowers are produced on long, trailing stems

Impatiens New Guinea Hybrid
These grow well in bright light and are ideal for planting in containers

MAINTAINING THE DISPLAY

Prune the barberry hard in late winter to encourage the growth of new shoots in spring. Regularly deadhead the impatiens, verbena, and roses in summer to ensure a continuous show of flowers. When the roots of the shrubs eventually become constricted, replace pot-bound plants with new specimens.

Rosa 'Simplex'
*Feed after pruning in
spring, and every two
weeks in midsummer*

*Beautiful flowers
of 'Simplex' have
slight fragrance*

*Windowbox is
9 in (23 cm)
deep to provide
sufficient soil mix
for roots of roses
and barberry*

*Limed wooden
windowbox
(see p. 105)
creates perfect
background for
trailing verbena*

TWIN PEAKS

Topiary makes a strong architectural statement and can bring a sense of formality to a setting. While clipped topiary requires time and an element of skill to achieve the required shape, ivy trained around a small metal frame will quickly produce a compact form. Its companion here, *Lysimachia nummularia* 'Aurea', is ideal for semi-shade, where a touch of sun will bring out the golden color of the leaves but not scorch them. *Bidens ferulifolia* is included for its pleasing combination of bright green leaves and yellow flowers.

YOU WILL NEED

1 *Hedera helix* 'Goldheart' (ivy)
   × 2, p.133
2 *Bidens ferulifolia* × 3, p.130
3 *Lysimachia nummularia* 'Aurea'
   (creeping Jenny,) × 3, p.135

Hedera helix 'Goldheart'
Once established, ivy will grow rapidly around wire frames

Bidens ferulifolia
Yellow, daisy-like flowers are produced at ends of long stems

Lysimachia nummularia 'Aurea'
Golden foliage can be encouraged to trail through other plants

2 ft 4 in (70 cm)

Metal frame placed at back of windowbox

MAINTAINING THE DISPLAY

Keep this summer arrangement tidy with regular trimming. Lightly prune the ivy to encourage bushy growth once it has worked its way around the topiary frame (see p. 121). The bidens will grow up to 2 ft (60 cm) in length; trim long stems regularly to keep them under control. Creeping Jenny will also benefit from cutting back, encouraging young growth that will produce the brightest leaves.

Since bidens is not frost hardy, consider replacing it with gold pansies for winter color

ROYAL PURPLE

Rich, royal purple was the inspiration for this summer arrangement, determining the choice of plants and the decoration of the windowbox. The flowers of *Verbena* 'Imagination' and the leaves of the ornamental clover *Trifolium repens* 'Purpurascens' are in the same shade, while woolly, silver-leaved *Stachys lanata*, creeping, white-flowered *Bacopa* 'Snowflake', and upright, gray-green *Ballota pseudodictamnus* provide a pale, soft contrast.

YOU WILL NEED

1 *Trifolium repens* 'Purpurascens'
  (purple-leaved clover)
  × 3, p.138
2 *Verbena* 'Imagination' × 4, p.139
3 *Stachys lanata* (lamb's ears)
  × 1, p.138
4 *Bacopa* 'Snowflake' × 2, p.129
5 *Ballota pseudodictamnus*
  × 2, p.129

MAINTAINING THE DISPLAY

The plants in this arrangement need little more than regular watering, feeding, and trimming. The lamb's ears and *Ballota* produce flowers that are insignificant and may clash with the main color interest of the display. As their flowers begin to form, remove the buds to encourage the plants to put all their energy into producing new leaves.

Verbena 'Imagination'
This perennial, usually grown as an annual, bears clusters of flowers throughout summer

Stachys lanata
Silver foliage draws attention to center of arrangement

2 ft 4 in (70 cm)

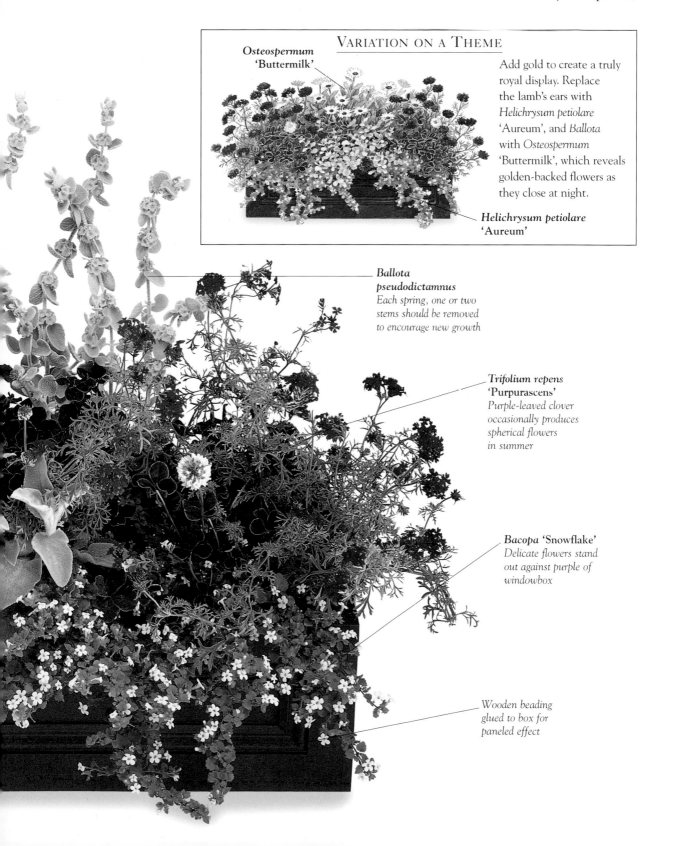

VARIATION ON A THEME

Osteospermum 'Buttermilk'

Add gold to create a truly royal display. Replace the lamb's ears with *Helichrysum petiolare* 'Aureum', and *Ballota* with *Osteospermum* 'Buttermilk', which reveals golden-backed flowers as they close at night.

Helichrysum petiolare 'Aureum'

Ballota pseudodictamnus
Each spring, one or two stems should be removed to encourage new growth

Trifolium repens 'Purpurascens'
Purple-leaved clover occasionally produces spherical flowers in summer

Bacopa 'Snowflake'
Delicate flowers stand out against purple of windowbox

Wooden beading glued to box for paneled effect

DESERT BOX

Creating a miniature
landscape in a windowbox can
be great fun. Here, the spiky,
bold shapes of cacti and other
succulents are suggestive of the
arid plains of New Mexico. The
classic cacti forms of *Opuntia*
and *Pachycereus* are contrasted
with the rounded compactness
of *Rebutia* and *Parodia*, while
the leaves of the succulent
aloes add a more angular shape.
A top-dressing of gravel adds
to the desert feel, and also
makes sound horticultural
sense, since it aids drainage and
helps to reduce moisture loss.

YOU WILL NEED

1 *Pachycereus schottii* (whisker cactus)
   × 1, p.136
2 *Aloe variegata* (partridge-breasted
   aloe) × 2, p.129
3 *Rebutia marsoneri* × 1, p.137
4 *Opuntia lindheimeri* (prickly pear)
   × 1, p.136
5 *Parodia graessneri* × 1, p.136

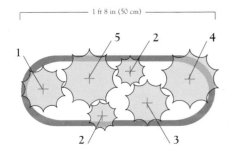

1 ft 8 in (50 cm)

Pachycereus schottii
*Growth of this
potentially large plant is
restricted by container*

*Pachycereus is
multi-stemmed*

*Top layer of gravel
is attractive
and prevents
growth of algae*

MAINTAINING THE DISPLAY

To ensure adequate drainage,
plant this arrangement in
three parts soil mix to one part
gravel. In summer, water only
when the potting material has
dried out. Water occasionally if
at all in cool conditions. Cacti
need a minimum temperature
of 55°F (13°C) to survive
outdoors. Bring the display
indoors before the first frosts,
and keep by a bright window.
Once new growth starts,
apply a commercial fertilizer.

Opuntia lindheimeri
*Flat pads grow quickly
on top of main stem*

*Orange and
red flowers
will grow on
edge of pad
in spring*

Aloe variegata
*Spikes of pink to
red flowers are
produced in spring*

Parodia graessneri
*Fine, sharp spines
cover surface*

**Rebutia
marsoneri**
*Yellow flowers
open by day
and close at night*

*Sand patterns have
been applied to
terracotta using
strong, clear,
liquid glue*

SHIMMERING SILVER & RED

Brilliant scarlet is such a striking, dominant color that some gardeners avoid it. Here, it is used with silver foliage and a galvanized metal container to create a bold, modern display. The vibrant *Petunia* 'Red Carpet' has green leaves, but the other flowering plants – *Lotus berthelotii*, with its flame-like flowers, and *Eschscholzia californica* 'Dali', with its papery, red blooms – have a hint of blue and silver in their foliage. The soft-textured, much-divided leaves of *Pyrethrum ptarmiciflorum* resemble silver filigree.

YOU WILL NEED

1 *Petunia* 'Red Carpet' × 2, p.137
2 *Lotus berthelotii* (fire vine) × 3, p.135
3 *Eschscholzia californica* 'Dali' (California poppy) × 4, p.132
4 *Pyrethrum ptarmiciflorum* 'Silver Feather' × 3, p.137

MAINTAINING THE DISPLAY

This arrangement will thrive in full sun. Petunias are liable to be damaged by rain and will benefit from a sheltered site. Deadhead the petunias and poppies regularly for a continuous display of flowers, and pinch out the buds on the pyrethrum to encourage the growth of fresh foliage.

Petunia 'Red Carpet'
Liquid fertilizer should be applied every two weeks while plant is in flower

Eschscholzia californica 'Dali'
This annual can be grown from seed in the windowbox in late spring

1 ft 9 in (53 cm)

Pyrethrum ptarmiciflorum
'Silver Feather'
*Leaves will survive mild winters
but can be damaged by excess rain*

*This variety of
California poppy
often shows a
yellow eye at
center of flower*

*Galvanized metal
windowbox
will not rust*

Lotus berthelotii
*Fire vine may not flower in
cool summers, but is worth
growing for its foliage alone*

Aromatic Herbs

It is a joy to use fresh herbs when cooking, and they will grow happily on a window-ledge. Herbs are attractive plants, too, with their striking foliage, flowers, and fragrance. Plant them in individual pots to provide each with the most suitable growing conditions – Mediterranean herbs, such as rosemary and basil, prefer free-draining soil mix and full sun, while mint and parsley like moist soil and a shady site.

You Will Need

1 *Allium schoenoprasum* (chives) × 1, p.129
2 *Rosmarinus officinalis* 'Severn Sea' (rosemary) × 1, p.138
3 *Salvia officinalis* 'Purpurascens' (purple sage) × 1, p.138
4 *Ocimum basilicum* (basil) × 1, p.136
5 *Origanum vulgare* 'Aureum' (golden marjoram) × 1, p.136
6 *Mentha suaveolens* 'Variegata' (pineapple mint) × 1, p.135
7 *Petroselinum crispum* var. *neapolitanum* (flat-leaved parsley) × 1, p.136

— 2 ft 10 in (85 cm) —

Maintaining the Display

Rosemary is evergreen and survives to slightly above freezing (32°F/0°C). Marjoram, chives, and mint (and, often, sage), kept in position on the windowledge, will die down and grow again in spring. Replace basil and parsley in late spring or, alternatively, bring them indoors for the winter, and place in a sunny room.

Allium schoenoprasum
Hollow chive leaves produce pleasant onion flavor

Rosmarinus officinalis 'Severn Sea'
Rosemary's spring flowers can be used in salads

Salvia officinalis 'Purpurascens'
Purple sage can be propagated by cuttings taken in late summer

Ocimum basilicum
Basil should be put outside only after danger of frost has passed

PRACTICAL SUGGESTION

Preserve some herbs for use out of season by drying their leaves. Pick them on a dry summer morning, when the leaves are full of flavor, tie into bundles, and hang them upside down in a warm, dry, shady place. Herbs such as basil and coriander are best frozen.

Sage

Rosemary

Mint

Parsley

Golden marjoram

Petroselinum crispum var. *neapolitanum*
A biennial usually grown as an annual, flat-leaved parsley has a better flavor than curly-leaved varieties

Mentha suaveolens 'Variegata'
Flower buds of mint should be cut off as they appear to encourage growth of new foliage

Mint is extremely invasive and is best grown on its own

In growing season, herbs should be fed every two weeks with liquid fertilizer

Terracotta pots are decorated with single coat of water-based paint

Origanum vulgare 'Aureum'
Golden marjoram needs partial shade to prevent scorch

RICH PURPLE & SILVER

Ornamental grasses are becoming an increasingly popular feature in gardens, and they also make striking container plants. Their slender, spiky foliage gives height, movement, and a welcome airiness to an arrangement. Here the silvery blue leaves of *Helictotrichon sempervirens* make a striking contrast with the round, felt-like leaves of *Helichrysum petiolare*. The trailing, white, summer blooms of petunias bring cool elegance to the display, while purple petunia flowers add drama.

YOU WILL NEED

1 *Helictotrichon sempervirens* (blue oat grass) × 1, p.133
2 *Convolvulus cneorum* × 2, p.131
3 *Helichrysum petiolare* 'Microphyllus' × 2, p.133
4 *Petunia* 'Brilliant White' × 4, p.136
5 *Petunia* 'Purple Wave' × 4, p.137

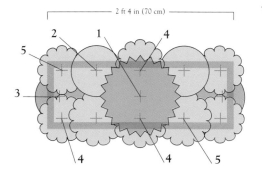

2 ft 4 in (70 cm)

MAINTAINING THE DISPLAY

Petunias bring vibrant color to this display – encourage bushy growth and a plentiful display of flowers in and around the windowbox by cutting back long stems and deadheading regularly. In late summer, prune straggly growth on the helichrysum back to a leaf joint to produce new, silvery growth.

Convolvulus cneorum
White, trumpet-shaped flowers close in evening

Helichrysum petiolare 'Microphyllus'
This shrub should be overwintered in sheltered, frost-free spot

Helictotrichon sempervirens
This grass produces tall, straw-colored flower spikes in summer

*Dead flower spikes of grass
are attractive and can be
left through winter, to
be cut down in spring*

ALTERNATIVE ARRANGEMENT

For a striking, modern arrangement, scatter drops of
silver paint onto a black windowbox, and plant it up
with a single species, such as a trailing petunia. Here,
the abundantly flowering, richly colored *Petunia*
'Purple Wave' cascades over its container.

*Bushy, silvery
convolvulus is
evergreen*

**Petunia
'Brilliant White'**
*Gray throat flares out
into pure white petals*

Petunia 'Purple Wave'
*Striking purple flowers
have a dark eye at center*

CONTRASTING FOLIAGE

Shade is often thought of as a second-best environment in which to grow plants. It is true that bright, large-flowered plants need sun, but shady areas provide a wonderful opportunity to grow attractive foliage. This summer arrangement contrasts the oval leaves of *Hosta ventricosa* with the frilly fronds of two ferns, *Phyllitis scolopendrium* 'Cristatum' and *Polystichum setiferum* 'Divisilobum'. Shade-loving *Mimulus luteus* is used for its glowing yellow flowers.

YOU WILL NEED

1 *Mimulus luteus* (monkeyflower)
  × 5, p.135
2 *Hosta ventricosa* var. *aureomaculata*
  (plantain lily) × 2, p.134
3 *Polystichum setiferum* 'Divisilobum'
  (soft shield fern) × 1, p.137
4 *Phyllitis scolopendrium* 'Cristatum'
  × 2, p.137

Mimulus luteus
This is one of few yellow-flowered annuals that thrives in shade

Phyllitis scolopendrium 'Cristatum'
Evergreen fronds are crinkled at edges

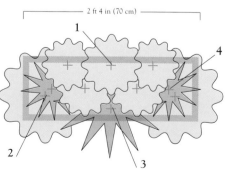

2 ft 4 in (70 cm)

Height of monkeyflower can be controlled by pinching out growing tips between fingers

ALTERNATIVE ARRANGEMENT

Lonicera nitida 'Baggesen's Gold'

Euonymus fortunei 'Emerald Gaiety'

Hedera helix 'Goldheart'

Mimulus luteus

For a semi-shady, formal arrangement in green and gold, try planting *Euonymus fortunei* 'Emerald Gaiety' with two *Lonicera nitida* 'Baggesen's Gold' clipped into globes. Train a swag of *Hedera helix* 'Goldheart' on garden wire across the front of the box, and add *Mimulus luteus* for summer color.

Polystichum setiferum **'Divisilobum'**
Feathery, evergreen fronds bring softening effect to center of box

Hosta ventricosa **var. aureomaculata**
Plantain lily produces bell-shaped, purple flower spikes in summer

Heart-shaped, green leaves of hosta are variegated with cream

Green and gold crackleglaze (see p. 107) echoes color scheme of planting

MAINTAINING THE DISPLAY
Hostas and ferns will perform best in a soil-based potting mix with added organic matter to retain moisture. Keep slugs and snails away from the hosta leaves by smearing petroleum jelly around the top of the container. Thin out some of the old fern fronds in spring as new fronds unfurl.

BUDGET BLUE BOX

This arrangement is both eye-catching and inexpensive. Its plastic trough is packed with annuals that are widely available or can be grown in position from seed. The planting combines several shades of blue, with pale and dark lobelias, delicate *Felicia bergeriana*, and vibrant *Anchusa capensis* 'Blue Angel'. To complete the theme and add an attractive shine, the box has been coated with blue gloss paint over an acrylic undercoat, which prevents the paint from flaking off.

YOU WILL NEED

1   *Lobelia* 'Crystal Palace' × 4, p.135
2   *Lobelia* 'Lilac Cascade' × 4, p.135
3   *Lobelia* 'Sapphire' × 1, p.135
4   *Anchusa capensis* 'Blue Angel'
    × 2, p.129
5   *Felicia bergeriana* (kingfisher daisy)
    × 2, p.133

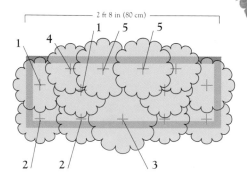

MAINTAINING THE DISPLAY
A mixed planting of annuals such as this is an excellent value, with the lobelias, in particular, staying in flower for months if they are well watered, fed, and trimmed back regularly (see p. 121). Pinch out the stalks as well as the flowers of the felicia to keep it neat. Feed all the plants every two weeks with a liquid fertilizer.

Anchusa capensis 'Blue Angel'
Small, bowl-shaped flowers attract bees

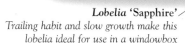

Lobelia 'Sapphire'
Trailing habit and slow growth make this lobelia ideal for use in a windowbox

Felicia bergeriana
*Daisy-like flowers open
in sunshine and close
if clouds appear*

ALTERNATIVE ARRANGEMENT

**Calendula
officinalis**

An abundance of annuals in
yellow is a cheerful contrast to
the blue of the windowbox.
*Limnanthes douglasii, Calendula
officinalis,* and *Tropaeolum* 'Tom
Thumb' are all easy to grow.

Tropaeolum 'Tom Thumb'

Limnanthes douglasii

Lobelia 'Crystal Palace'
*Compact habit introduces
clumps of color to
center of display*

**Lobelia
'Lilac Cascade'**
*Delicate flowers hang
from trailing stems*

*Combination of deep blue petals
and white centers of this lobelia
contrasts with single-color flowers*

ICE-CREAM BOX

The variation between shades of white in this single-color planting is strikingly effective. The ice of *Viola cornuta alba* contrasts with the cream of *Antirrhinum majus* 'White Wonder', while the golden throat of the petunia's trumpet adds a warmth to its pure white flower. *Tradescantia fluminensis* 'Albovittata', with its cool, white-and-green variegated foliage, is usually grown as a houseplant but can be planted outdoors in the summer. The rich cream of the wooden windowbox is the ideal foil for this profusion of white flowers.

YOU WILL NEED

1 *Antirrhinum majus* 'White Wonder' (snapdragon) × 5, p.129
2 *Viola cornuta alba* (horned violet) × 3, p.139
3 *Petunia* 'Brilliant White' × 3, p.136
4 *Tradescantia fluminensis* 'Albovittata' (wandering Jew) × 2, p.138

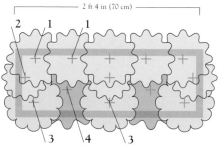

2 ft 4 in (70 cm)

Antirrhinum majus 'White Wonder'
This snapdragon grows well in containers, flowering freely for weeks in summer

Tradescantia fluminensis 'Albovittata'
Repotted, this can be used as a houseplant throughout winter

Cuttings of tradescantia can be taken for new arrangements (see p. 122)

MAINTAINING THE DISPLAY

To encourage a long flowering season, regularly pinch out dead petunia flowerheads, and cut the spikes of faded snapdragon flowers close to the base for a second flush. In autumn, replace them with dwarf white narcissi for spring color, and trim back the violas.

Viola cornuta alba
This delicate perennial will flourish year after year

Petunia
'Brilliant White'
Trailing habit of this variety makes it perfect for use in windowboxes and hanging baskets

STRIKING SINGLES

For a simple but striking arrangement in a windowbox, it is hard to beat a bold mass of flowers in a single color, gloriously demonstrated in this planting by the rich yellow, double flowers of *Begonia elatior* 'Yellow'. The planting is so simple that you can afford to be adventurous when planning the decoration of the container. Here, a plain wooden windowbox has been brightened up with an application of small mosaic tiles in rich blue and gold, laid in a random pattern. When deciding on a color scheme, match or contrast the arrangement with the decorated windowbox to create an impressive display.

MAINTAINING THE DISPLAY

This begonia is easily raised from seed and flowers freely in shade or semi-shade throughout the summer. In autumn, dig up the tubers that will have formed, dry them thoroughly, removing all traces of growth, and store them in an unheated room in dry sand or soil mix. In spring, plant the tubers in individual pots filled with soil mix, and water. Once new growth appears, start feeding the begonias, and plant them outside when all danger of frost has passed.

Begonia elatior 'Yellow'
Double blooms resemble camellia flowers

Flowers can be pinched out as they begin to fade

YOU WILL NEED

1   *Begonia elatior* 'Yellow' × 5, p.129

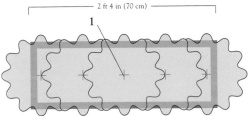

2 ft 4 in (70 cm)

1

ALTERNATIVE ARRANGEMENT

Positioned in a sunny site, the perennial *Nolana* 'Blue Bird' makes a perfect single-species planting for this gold-and-blue, mosaic window-box. Masses of sky blue, trumpet-like flowers with white throats bloom throughout the summer and trail softly over the edges of the container. Nolana can easily be grown from seed (see p. 123).

Glossy leaves highlight golden blooms

Leggy stems should be cut back to promote bushy, new growth

Waterproof tile adhesive secures mosaic tiles to box (see p. 107)

CREATIVE PLANTING

SPRING VARIETY
A range of containers, including
treated wicker baskets, displays mainly
spring-flowering bulbs, such as tulips,
daffodils, and hyacinths.

Container gardening offers a marvelous opportunity
to grow a wide range of plants suitable for many
different locations and climates. A small site and a limited
number of plants are an ideal starting point for some
truly creative planting, experimenting with colors and
textures for a traditional or a refreshingly contemporary
style, using groups of plants, such as ornamental grasses,
succulents, and climbers, that have not been widely
associated with containers in the past.

SUNNY TERRACOTTA
The rich color and smooth lines of
these terracotta pots are the perfect
foil for the gold, silver, white, and
green tones of the planting.

DESIGNING WITH PLANTS

The first step when creating a container garden is to assess the site carefully, enabling you to choose plants that will thrive in those conditions. Determine which areas are in shade or semi-shade and which receive full sun. Protection from the elements is an important factor, too. Decide whether the site can provide winter protection for tender plants or, on a roof or balcony, shelter from the wind. In addition to these practical considerations, bear in mind the mood that you would like to create – lush, green, and tranquil, coolly formal, or hot and exotic, for example.

Every location offers an opportunity for planting, so be inventive and make good use of the space that is available. Hang baskets from brackets on walls, place pots on stairs and on front doorsteps, and place boxes on windowledges. If there are no ledges, mount a half-basket or box supported on brackets to the wall below the window. Railings make ideal supports for climbing plants, but if they serve as banisters on steps, avoid rampant growers in order to keep the handrail clear.

Consider the surrounding environment, too. Decide which views are attractive and would benefit from being framed by a planting, and which are unsightly and should be screened.

PERFECT SUMMER COMPANIONS
The muted, subtle tones of silver-gray and blue-green succulents and the delicate, pale pink, trailing geraniums complement this flight of lichen-encrusted stone steps leading up to a similarly weathered, wooden front door.

AN ENTRANCE FRAMED WITH COLOR
The irregularly shaped heads of two standard roses and the mixed plantings down each side of these steps soften a grand door and give a warm, welcoming feel to what would otherwise appear to be an imposing formal entrance.

MEDITERRANEAN-STYLE STAIRWAY
The textured, ochre walls of this building are recognizably Mediterranean in style. This impression is reinforced with carefully chosen, sun-loving plants, positioned to utilize all available space. Geraniums, in a range of vivid colors and a mixture of terracotta pots, run up the stairs. A rubber plant and papyrus introduce contrasting foliage shapes and colors.

BLOSSOMING BASKET BY A DOOR
This lush summer basket, hung at eye level, is a perfect welcome for visitors. Crisp white, double, tuberous begonias reflect the color of the front door, while the violet-blue lobelia, yellow daisy-like bidens, and golden helichrysum add warmth and brightness to the arrangement.

COLOR AND TEXTURE IN AN UNPROMISING SPACE

This pleasant jumble of containers and plants works well, making use of what would otherwise be an unused space beside a flight of stairs. Tables, plant stands, and plinths raise the containers to different levels. Features such as the wall plaque and garden bench anchor *the eye and add interest. Plain green and variegated ivies, helichrysum, boxwood, and a yucca introduce a range of leaf sizes and shapes, while annual bedding plants such as geraniums, osteospermums, and petunias provide bursts of welcome color.*

PLANTING IN SHADE

If your site is partially or entirely enclosed, it is important that you make a note of the areas that are in shade at different times of the day. This will vary through the year, since the sun completes a high arc in summer and a low arc in winter, casting long shadows. The position of surrounding objects, such as a tree or building, may result in the site being almost completely in shade. While the prospect of growing plants in such a place may seem a daunting one initially, there is a range of attractive plants to choose from that thrive in these conditions. In addition, many practical improvements can be made to lighten a dark area.

PRACTICAL ALTERATIONS

Before positioning your planted-up containers, maximize available daylight by painting walls white, cream, or soft yellow, using a paint that is suitable for the surface. Make sure that the paint adheres to the surface by brushing

PAVING MATERIALS

The surface used to pave an area will form an integral part of a display, so it is important to ensure that its texture and color complement the surroundings. Choose a symmetrical or irregular design to harmonize or contrast with the display. For an entrance or patio, choose artificial stone or textured concrete, since these are less expensive than real stone. For a balcony or roof garden, select a lightweight material.

Concrete slab

Artificial stone paving

Sandstone slab

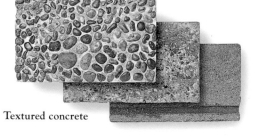

Textured concrete

off loose material and applying a primer. Choose a pale-colored paving material for the ground. Use waterproofed mirrors to reflect available daylight, and position them so that they bounce light into dark corners. Install artificial lighting, since a dark area should be illuminated for safety. Angle the lights to pick out details in the planting.

FLOWERS AND FOLIAGE

Among the plants that do well in shade are those that are grown primarily for their foliage, such as ferns and hostas. For year-round interest in all but the coldest regions, choose evergreens with glossy leaves that reflect light, such as *Fatsia japonica* and camellia, or those with bright, variegated foliage, such as ivy, holly, and *Euonymus fortunei*. A number of flowering plants tolerate shade. Suitable plants for spring include primroses and woodland bulbs, such as *Anemone blanda* and dog's-tooth violets; in summer, begonias, mimulus, and flowering tobacco; and in autumn, pansies and cyclamen. Plants with white or very pale pink flowers stand out well in shade.

SHADY ENTRANCE PROJECT

This plan reduces the three dimensions of a site to two, offering a design for a shady entrance. It highlights available planting areas such as steps and a windowledge and features arrangements that will make the most of their location. The fall of sun and shade is shown, as are the design details used to improve the sense of light and space.

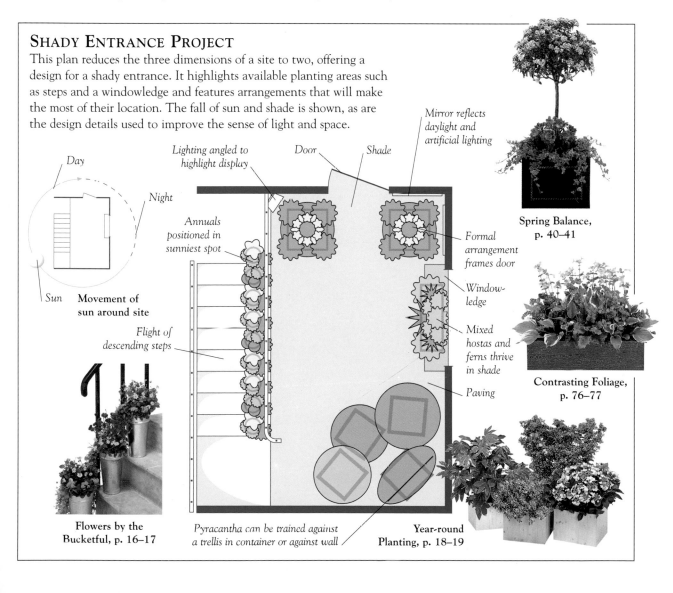

Day

Night

Sun **Movement of sun around site**

Annuals positioned in sunniest spot

Flight of descending steps

Lighting angled to highlight display

Door

Shade

Mirror reflects daylight and artificial lighting

Spring Balance, p. 40–41

Formal arrangement frames door

Window-ledge

Mixed hostas and ferns thrive in shade

Paving

Contrasting Foliage, p. 76–77

Flowers by the Bucketful, p. 16–17

Pyracantha can be trained against a trellis in container or against wall

Year-round Planting, p. 18–19

PLANTING IN A SUNNY SITE

The range of plants that thrives in full sun is virtually limitless. To simplify your choice, restrict the number of plants under consideration by deciding on a theme. This could be based on color, shape, or texture, or on a mood such as Mediterranean.

Plants with bright blooms are generally sun-lovers, and colors such as orange and scarlet are intensified by strong light. Annuals are justifiably popular, but use evergreen perennials and shrubs for a continuous display.

LOW-MAINTENANCE CHOICE

Desert plants, including succulents and cacti, look good in the harsh light of direct sun, casting dramatic shadows of their exotic forms. These are ideal for a hot, sunny location since they are drought resistant and require a minimal amount of watering.

Most container plants that are positioned in a sunny spot will need to be watered regularly to prevent their compost from drying out (see p. 118).

SUNNY DECK PROJECT

This plan suggests plantings for a site that receives direct sun throughout the day. Geraniums and succulents are placed against a wall, which will provide shelter from cold and wind. Moving away from the building, the displays become tall and pretty, with delicate flowers and textured foliage. These arrangements soften the site's boundaries and supply an element of privacy.

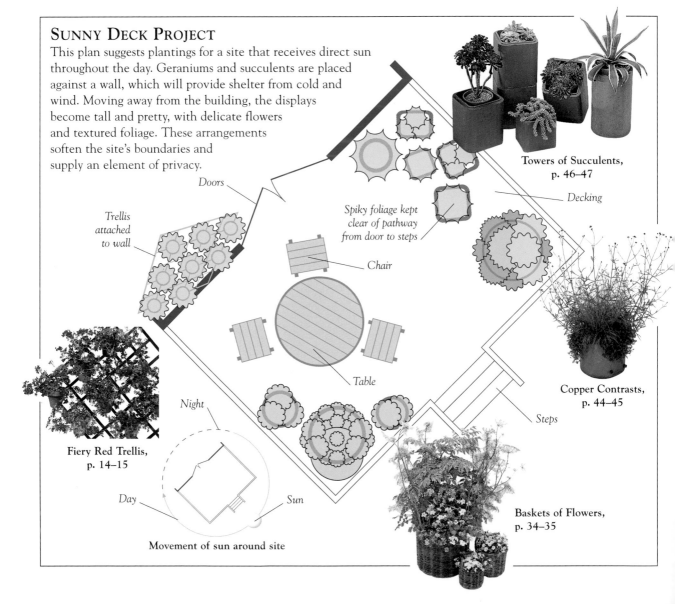

Doors

Trellis attached to wall

Spiky foliage kept clear of pathway from door to steps

Chair

Table

Night

Day

Sun

Movement of sun around site

Fiery Red Trellis, p. 14–15

Towers of Succulents, p. 46–47

Decking

Copper Contrasts, p. 44–45

Steps

Baskets of Flowers, p. 34–35

DRAMATIC FORMS ON A WOODEN DECK

The clever use of driftwood lends an Oriental feel to this simple group of cacti and succulents. The muted, natural colors of the pots add to the overall organic look of the arrangement, which is complemented by the surrounding varnished wood.

A FOCAL POINT IN A SMALL SPACE

A panel of trompe l'oeil trellis provides a focus for an almost bare wall, and helps to separate visually the topiary standard globe from the climbing ivy. The false perspective of the trellis also gives a sense of vistas beyond the confines of the garden.

WOODEN DECKING

An attractive alternative to paving, wooden decking can be laid in a variety of different patterns. Hardwoods, such as redwood and red cedar, are ideal, since they do not need to be treated with preservative. Softwoods, such as spruce and pine, are not as durable but can be used if treated to resist rot. Take care, since decking can become slippery if wet.

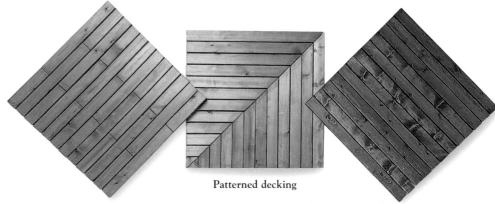

Clear sealed decking

Patterned decking

Stained decking

PLANTING IN AN EXPOSED SITE

The most common problems encountered in an exposed site are caused by strong, gusty winds. The key to growing plants successfully in such conditions lies in protecting them from the elements, ideally without dramatically reducing any potential views. In addition, if you have room, consider providing a sheltered seating area.

Initially, you will need to create a wind barrier around the perimeters of the site. Permeable barriers that filter the wind, such as a trellis, woven hurdle, or softwood lattice fencing, are more successful at reducing the wind's force than solid barriers that attempt to block it out, but instead cause swirling eddies that can damage the plants.

TOUGH SPECIMENS

Plants need to be sturdy to cope with exposed conditions. Those with leathery, evergreen foliage, such as ivy and mahonia, are particularly suitable. Mahonia is an ideal plant for an exposed site, since it also has narrow, jagged leaves through which the wind can whistle. Plants with twiggy, open habits and small leaves, such as contorted hazel, can withstand the wind because it passes straight through them, while flexible grasses bend

ROOFTOP HAVEN
This roof garden has been transformed into a delightful seating area. A pergola provides privacy, and evergreen foliage surrounds the edge of the site, creating a long season of interest.

with the breeze rather than break. Low-growing plants, such as lobelia, sweet alyssum, and *Bacopa*, also offer little resistance to wind.

Strong winds and sun will cause the soil mix in a pot to dry out quickly. A container made from a nonporous material, such as plastic, fiberglass, or metal, will retain moisture more effectively than a porous type, so will need less watering. These materials are also lightweight – an important factor on a roof or balcony.

WINDY ROOF GARDEN PROJECT

This plan suggests plantings for a site above ground level that is exposed to wind. A trellis has been erected for privacy and shelter, and evergreen *Euonymus* and ivy is grown through it. A mixture of sun and shade provides an opportunity for different displays. The illusion of additional space is created by positioning a group of containers to screen off the seating area from the building.

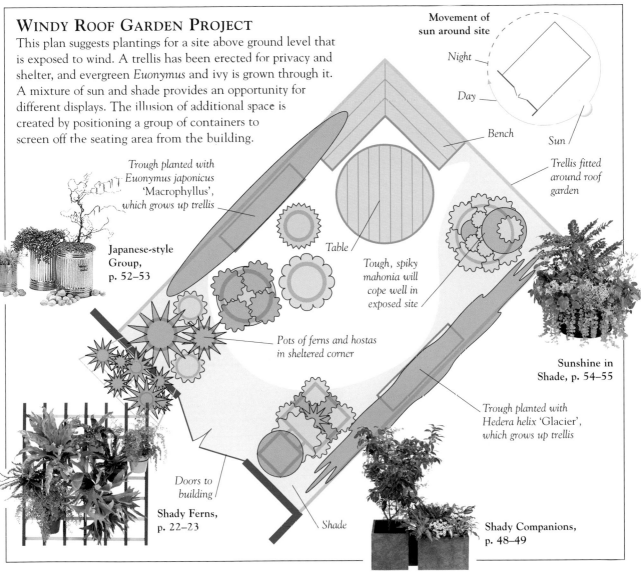

Movement of sun around site

Night

Day

Bench

Sun

Trellis fitted around roof garden

Trough planted with *Euonymus japonicus* 'Macrophyllus', which grows up trellis

Japanese-style Group, p. 52–53

Table

Tough, spiky mahonia will cope well in exposed site

Pots of ferns and hostas in sheltered corner

Sunshine in Shade, p. 54–55

Trough planted with *Hedera helix* 'Glacier', which grows up trellis

Doors to building

Shady Ferns, p. 22–23

Shade

Shady Companions, p. 48–49

TRELLIS AND FENCING

The choice of trellis or fencing will depend on the style of container garden that you are creating. A square or diamond trellis will suit a formal setting and is an ideal support for a climber, while a country atmosphere can be achieved using woven hurdles or softwood lattice fencing. Ensure that all panels are attached to supporting posts.

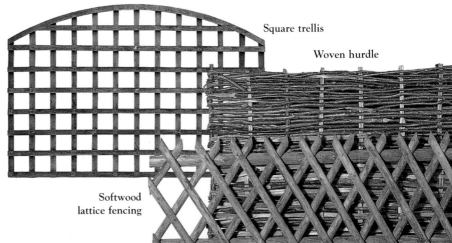

Square trellis

Woven hurdle

Softwood lattice fencing

STYLING A DISPLAY

Once you have determined which plants will thrive in a particular site, you can begin to consider the mood that you wish to create. For instance, do you long for a lush, green, cool oasis, or would you prefer to create a suntrap with sizzling, hot colors? Does stark, dramatic foliage appeal, or is a profusion of pretty flowers more suited to the setting?

Certain types of plant can be used to evoke different styles. Summer bedding such as petunias, geraniums, lobelia, and helichrysum have long been planted in containers; group them to form a familiar, traditional display. Alternatively, some plants are particularly suited to a contemporary style. Create clean lines, architectural forms, and dramatic shapes with a careful selection of shrubs, perennials, succulents, and grasses.

USING COLOR

Flowers and foliage are available in every color of the rainbow, as well as in white and black. Within each band of color

ARCHITECTURAL FOLIAGE
Combined with an elegant planter that has been treated with a verdigris paint finish (see p. 106), the ribbed, blue-green leaves of Hosta sieboldii 'Elegans' would make a strong contribution to a contemporary display.

there are so many shades that planning a display is rather like painting with plants, and your reaction to a finished arrangement will be a very personal one. It is possible to combine many shades in one display, but for a harmonious planting design use a limited number of colors that blend or contrast with each other. Pink, blue, and silver is a popular combination, since the effect is soft and relaxing. A mix of blue, yellow, and white is fresh and crisp. An arrangement in a single color can also work extremely well; an all-white planting with fresh green foliage, for instance, looks cool and elegant.

STRIKING CENTERPIECE
This lovely, weathered stone urn is perfect for a traditional planting design. Brilliant white petunias surround a fresh green, clipped boxwood, and silver helichrysum trails over the edges to soften the contours of the container.

Alternatively, combining bright red flowers and silver leaves results in a striking, contemporary look. Consider creating a display using only foliage plants – their colors range from reds and purples to greens infused with silver, gold, and creamy white.

USING FOLIAGE

A variety of foliage plants can be used to spectacular effect in traditional and contemporary plantings. Think about outline, shape, and the shadows that will be cast. Sharp contrasts of leaf shapes, such as a fern with its delicate fronds placed next to a hosta with solid, rounded leaves, form an eye-catching display. Ornamental grasses are increasingly popular garden plants and thrive in containers – their light, airy foliage adds welcome movement and height to an arrangement.

MATCHING TONES
This bright, spring windowbox shows that a two-color scheme need not be dull. White and yellow flowers of narcissi and pansies are combined with the plain green and variegated foliage of ivies, Aucuba japonica, and dwarf conifers. This color scheme is continued in the plantings positioned below the windowbox.

AROMATIC CULINARY BASKET
Where space is limited, a large hanging basket planted with sun-loving, fragrant herbs such as basil, chives, marjoram, and chamomile is useful for cooking, as well as decorative. Ideally, this type of basket should be positioned beside a kitchen window.

BRILLIANTLY COLORFUL DISPLAY
In this autumn arrangement for a windowledge, a number of contrasting colors has been successfully combined. Bright yellow cherry peppers and purple petunias coexist happily with scarlet and magenta cyclamen. In theory, the colors in this planting should clash, but they are so strong that each holds its own against the others, creating a pleasing, vibrant display.

FINDING THE RIGHT PLANT

This quick-reference chart is intended to help you design with plants, giving details such as growth, tolerance of climate, and season of interest. Use the headings running along the top of the chart to isolate the type of plant that you are looking for, then scan down the vertical list of names to choose a specific plant. All the plants included here are described further in the *Plant Index* (see p. 128–139). The various cultivars of a plant are indicated by "cvs."

PLANTS	Low-maintenance	Fast-growing	Long-flowering	Scented flowers or foliage	Architectural foliage
Abutilon 'Orangeade'		●	●		
Acanthus mollis	●				●
Adiantum raddianum	●				
Agave americana 'Variegata'	●				●
Ageratum cvs.			●		
Argyranthemum frutescens		●	●		
Asplenium nidus	●				
Asplenium scolopendrium	●				
Bacopa 'Snowflake'		●	●		
Begonia pendula cvs.		●	●		
Begonia × tuberhybrida cvs.		●	●		
Bidens ferulifolia		●	●		
Blechnum spicant	●				
Brachyscome multifida	●	●	●		
Bracteantha bracteata 'Bright Bikini'			●		
Buxus sempervirens	●				●
Calendula officinalis	●				
Camellia japonica 'Alba Simplex'	●				
Carex comans 'Bronze Form'	●	●			●
Choisya ternata 'Sundance'				●	
Clematis flammula		●		●	●
Convolvulus cneorum	●		●		
Convolvulus sabatius syn. C. mauritanicus		●	●		
Cordyline australis 'Torbay Dazzler'	●				●
Corylus avellana 'Contorta'	●				●
Crocosmia cvs.					●
Diascia rigescens			●		
Eccremocarpus scaber		●	●		●
Eschscholzia californica cvs.					

AUTHOR'S TOP 10 PLANTS FOR CONTAINERS

The plants that I use again and again all have the longest possible season of interest. *Bidens ferulifolia*, for example, produces golden, daisy-like flowers throughout the summer and has lovely, airy foliage, while evergreen *Helichrysum petiolare* is perfect for softening an arrangement. *Acanthus mollis* is as valuable for its large, sculptural, semi-evergreen leaves as for its mauve and white flowers. Patio roses are marvelous in containers; *Rosa* 'Simplex' bears a profusion of rich pink flowers. Verbenas, particularly 'Peaches and Cream', are striking, as are sedges such as *Carex comans* 'Bronze Form'. In shade, *Fatsia japonica*, with its architectural, evergreen leaves, variegated *Euonymus fortunei* cultivars, and ivies are excellent, while impatiens flower for months.

Trailing	Shade-tolerant	Drought-tolerant	Wind-tolerant	Hot colors	Cool colors	Season of interest	Type
				Orange-red		Summer/autumn	Shrub
	●					All year	Perennial
	●					All year	Fern
		●	●			All year	Succulent
	●		●	Warm pink	White/blue	Summer	Annual
					White	Summer	Perennial
	●					All year	Fern
	●					All year	Fern
●			●		White	Summer/autumn	Annual
●	●			Yellow/red	White/pink	Summer/autumn	Tuber
	●			Yellow/red	White/pink	Summer/autumn	Tuber
●	●			Yellow		Summer/autumn	Perennial
	●		●			All year	Fern
		●	●	Warm pink	White/blue	Summer/autumn	Annual
				Yellow/orange/red		Summer/autumn	Annual
	●	●	●			All year	Shrub
			●	Yellow/orange		Summer	Annual
	●				White	Spring	Shrub
●		●	●	Bronze		All year	Sedge
	●	●		Yellow		Summer/autumn	Shrub
	●				White	Late summer	Shrub
		●	●		White	Summer/autumn	Shrub
●		●			Purple-blue	Summer/autumn	Perennial
		●	●	Bronze-cream		All year	Tree
			●			Winter/spring	Shrub
		●		Yellow/orange/red		Late summer	Corm
				Warm pink	Pale pink	Summer	Perennial
				Orange		Summer/autumn	Perennial
		●	●	Yellow-red		Summer	Annual

PLANTS	Low-maintenance	Fast-growing	Long-flowering	Scented flowers or foliage	Architectural foliage
Euonymus fortunei cvs.	●				
Fargesia murieliae 'Simba'		●			●
Fatsia japonica					●
Felicia amelloides	●		●		
Fuchsia (basket varieties)					
Gaillardia pulchella 'Red Plume'	●		●		
Glechoma hederacea 'Variegata'	●	●			
Hedera helix cvs.	●	●			●
Helichrysum petiolare	●	●			
Hosta cvs.	●				●
Hyacinthus orientalis 'L'Innocence'				●	
Impatiens cvs.	●		●		
Imperata cylindrica 'Rubra'	●				
Lantana 'Aloha'			●		
Lobelia pendula cvs.		●	●		
Lonicera nitida cvs.				●	
Lotus berthelotii	●				
Lysimachia nummularia 'Aurea'	●	●			
Mahonia japonica	●			●	●
Mimulus luteus, M. 'Viva'		●	●		
Miscanthus sinensis cvs.	●				●
Muscari botryoides 'Album'				●	
Nicotiana 'Lime Green'				●	
Osteospermum 'Buttermilk'			●		
Pelargonium (ivy-leaved varieties)			●		
Petunia cvs.		●	●		
Phormium tenax 'Bronze Baby'	●				●
Phyllitis scolopendrium 'Cristatum'	●				
Platycerium bifurcatum	●				●
Polystichum setiferum 'Divisilobum'	●				
Pyracantha 'Teton'					
Rosa			●	●	
Rosmarinus officinalis cvs.	●			●	
Sedum morganianum		●			●
Tropaeolum			●		
Tulipa 'Queen of Night'					
Tulipa 'Showwinner'					
Viburnum tinus	●				●
Yucca filamentosa	●			●	●

Trailing	Shade-tolerant	Drought-tolerant	Wind-tolerant	Hot colors	Cool colors	Season of interest	Type
	●					All year	Shrub
	●					All year	Bamboo
	●					All year	Shrub
		●	●		Blue	Summer	Perennial
●	●			Red	White/purple/pink	Summer	Shrub
				Red		Summer/autumn	Annual
●	●	●	●			All year	Perennial
●	●	●	●			All year	Perennial
●			●		Gray	All year	Shrub
	●					Summer/autumn	Perennial
	●				White	Spring	Bulb
	●		●	Orange/red/pink	White	Summer	Annual/perennial
			●	Red		Summer/autumn	Grass
	●		●	Yellow		Summer	Shrub
●	●		●	Red/pink	White/blue/lilac	Summer/autumn	Annual
	●	●	●		White	Spring	Shrub
●		●		Orange-red		Summer/autumn	Perennial
●	●	●	●	Yellow		All year	Perennial
	●		●	Yellow		All year	Shrub
	●			Yellow/red		Summer/autumn	Perennial
			●			All year	Grass
					White	Spring	Bulb
	●				Lime green	Summer	Annual
		●			Pale yellow	Summer/autumn	Perennial
●		●		Orange/red	White/pink	Summer	Perennial
●				Yellow/red/pink	White/purple	Summer/autumn	Annual
		●	●			All year	Perennial
	●		●			All year	Fern
●	●					All year	Fern
	●					All year	Fern
		●	●		White	All year	Shrub
				Yellow/orange/red	White/pink	Summer	Shrub
		●	●		Blue	All year	Shrub
●	●	●		Red		All year	Succulent
●	●		●	Yellow/orange/red		Summer/autumn	Annual
					Purple-black	Spring	Bulb
				Red		Spring	Bulb
	●	●	●		White/pink	All year	Shrub
		●	●		White	All year	Perennial

CONTAINER & PLANT CARE

A BURST OF SUMMER SUN
This golden arrangement, with its
combination of annuals, evergreen and
deciduous shrubs, and its deep blue,
ceramic containers, is a striking example
of a low-maintenance display.

Gardening in containers is a pleasure, not a chore.
Selecting, decorating, or even constructing a
container provides an opportunity to be creative, while
routine maintenance, such as deadheading, watering, and
feeding, brings you into regular contact with your plants.
Unlike a garden, a pot needs no digging or weeding, so
time can be devoted to getting to know the habits of your
plants, keeping them healthy, and enjoying their display.

KITCHEN COMBINATION
A simple planting such as this
requires little more than free-draining
soil mix, a sunny spot, and regular
watering to keep it flourishing.

CHOOSING A CONTAINER

The perfect combination of plants and pot makes all the difference between an arrangement that is ordinary and one that is stunning. There is a wide variety of containers available in a range of prices, materials, sizes, and styles. When making your choice, a key factor to bear in mind is the setting of the arrangement: ornate, antique stone urns look wonderful outside large, traditional houses, while simple shapes in terracotta, wood, or metal are most likely to suit smaller, modern buildings. If you have a balcony or roof garden, practical concerns such as weight are also important.

SYNTHETIC MATERIALS

The quality of containers made from synthetic materials has improved enormously in recent years. There are now excellent reproduction terracotta, lead, stone, and wooden containers that look genuine and have the advantage over natural materials of being light, inexpensive, durable, and requiring little maintenance.

Fiberglass box

Plastic planter

PLASTIC AND FIBERGLASS CONTAINERS

These containers are ideal for roof gardens and balconies where weight should be kept to a minimum, but avoid planting up with top-heavy specimens, since the wind may blow the arrangement over. Plastic is less expensive than fiberglass but is just as useful.

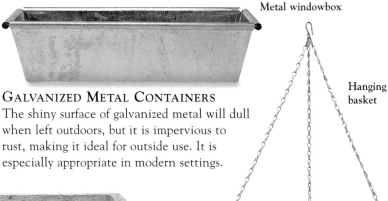

Metal windowbox

Hanging basket

GALVANIZED METAL CONTAINERS

The shiny surface of galvanized metal will dull when left outdoors, but it is impervious to rust, making it ideal for outside use. It is especially appropriate in modern settings.

Reconstituted stone trough

RECONSTITUTED STONE AND CONCRETE TUBS

Concrete and weathered, reconstituted stone containers are almost as attractive as real stone, and are less expensive. To give a new container an aged look, paint it with yogurt, sour milk, or liquid manure to encourage the growth of algae and lichens.

WIRE CONTAINERS

Plastic-coated wire containers, such as hanging and bracket baskets, are durable and light. Their wire frames make it easy to plant through the sides, creating a ball of flowers.

NATURAL MATERIALS

Containers made from natural materials, such as stone, wood, or terracotta, are a pleasing complement to a plant display, and the older they become, the better they look. Choose a simple planting design that shows off the beauty of the container, rather than hides it beneath trailing greenery.

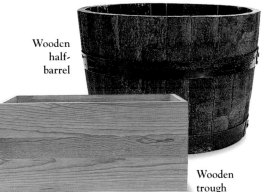

Wooden half-barrel

Wooden trough

WOODEN CONTAINERS

Wooden containers range from rustic half-barrels to sophisticated, planed wooden troughs, treated with plant-friendly wood preservative and decorated with colored woodstain or paint effects. In damp conditions, choose rot-resistant hardwood from a sustainable source.

Large terracotta planter

Weathered terracotta urn

TERRACOTTA PLANTERS

Hand-made terracotta pots are beautiful but expensive, so make sure that a container is guaranteed as frost-proof before buying it. Machine-made terracotta is attractive untreated or painted in bright colors. Both types will weather with age.

Terracotta windowbox

Ornate stone urn

STONE POTS

Used in the right setting, weathered stone containers help to give a garden an established feeling. They are extremely heavy, and careful thought should be given to their permanent position before planting up. A stone tub or urn will provide a stable base for a large plant, such as a tall shrub or small tree.

IMPROVISED CONTAINERS

Galvanized metal trashcan

Basket treated with varnish
(see p. 117)

Wicker basket

Any container may be used for planting, provided that you can protect it against the elements and make drainage holes in its base. For example, baskets and trashcans can be adapted for use.

WORKING WITH WOOD & METAL

It is relatively easy to make a wooden windowbox, especially if a lumber yard can cut the wood to size. Make sure that the box is at least 6–8 in (15–20 cm) wide and deep, and select a length appropriate to the location. Use marine or exterior-grade plywood if you plan to paint or stain the box. Treat wood such as cedar with clear varnish, or lime it to enhance the grain. Galvanized metal also makes an attractive container, particularly when it is planted up with a contemporary arrangement. Make drainage holes using a special bit for drilling metal.

CONSTRUCTING A WOODEN WINDOWBOX

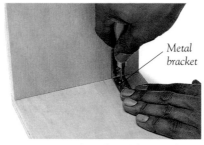

Metal bracket

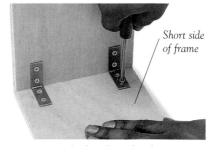

Short side of frame

1 *Construct the sides of the window-box first, using two metal brackets to secure each joint. With a sharp tool such as an awl, make a small hole to mark the position of each screw.*

2 *Fasten the brackets firmly into position. Leave the screws on one of the short sides of the frame until last, giving you plenty of room to maneuver with a screwdriver.*

3 *Attach four metal brackets to the base, two on each of the long sides. Slip the frame onto the base, mark the position for the screws with an awl, and screw them in tightly.*

Bracket fitted to base of box

MAKING A FRAME FOR A PLASTIC WINDOWBOX

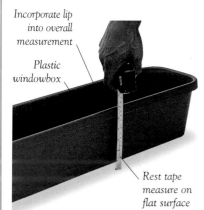

Incorporate lip into overall measurement

Plastic windowbox

Rest tape measure on flat surface

A plastic windowbox is practical and inexpensive, and its appearance can be improved with a wooden frame. Measure the height, width, and depth of the windowbox, adding ½ in (1 cm) to each measurement to determine the size of the frame. Build the frame (see Steps 1 and 2, above), without a base. Treat with exterior-grade gloss paint, waterproof varnish, or wood preservative, depending on the finish you wish to achieve.

Drill at slow speed for accuracy

4 *Turn the box upside down, and drill three ½-in (1-cm) drainage holes in the base. If the box is less than 2 ft (60 cm) long, drill two holes only. Paint the inside – including the holes – with plant-friendly wood preservative.*

DRILLING DRAINAGE HOLES IN A METAL CONTAINER

Position tape inside box

1 To allow for adequate drainage, drill a maximum of three holes in the base of a metal container. Place a piece of tape over the site of each hole to prevent the drill from slipping and causing damage.

Use bit for drilling metal

2 Place the container on sturdy supports, such as bricks, to raise it off the ground. Drill through the base from inside to avoid creating jagged holes that could clog up with soil mix. Use this method for plastic containers, too.

VARNISHING WOOD

1 To prepare a wooden container for varnish, rub the surface down using a fine-grade sandpaper. Always work in the direction of the grain to avoid scratches. Wipe away any dust.

2 Apply a coat of varnish, working in the direction of the grain. Allow to dry, then sand the surface. Add two further coats of varnish, sanding the surface between the applications.

LIMING A WOODEN CONTAINER

1 Work over the surface of the wood with a wire brush to open up the grain. Brush in the same direction as the grain, not across it, to avoid making scratches that will show up later.

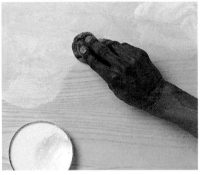

2 Apply liming paste or wax with fine steel wool, working into the grooves of the wood in a circular motion. Allow to dry for a few minutes. The effect may look patchy at this stage.

3 To remove the excess paste or wax, use a piece of clean, fine steel wool and a clear furniture polish, such as beeswax, and rub over the surface in a circular motion. Allow the container to dry for approximately 15 minutes, then buff the surface with a soft, lint-free cloth to give the container a slight sheen. If the surface begins to shows signs of wear, apply a fresh coat of furniture polish.

DECORATING CONTAINERS

Almost any container can be transformed into an attractive addition to your home. Achieve bright, bold effects with exterior gloss or acrylic paints. For something more adventurous but almost as easy, consider a decorative paint finish. Alternatively, create a mosaic with simple tiling. Always ensure that the surface of the container is correctly prepared: treat wood and metal with the appropriate primer, and apply an acrylic base coat to plastic in order to create a surface onto which paint can adhere. Improve the durability of wood with three coats of clear, waterproof varnish.

CREATING A VERDIGRIS PAINT FINISH

1 *A simple verdigris paint finish can be applied to any container. First make sure that the surface has been primed. Apply a base coat of matte olive-green paint, and allow it to dry.*

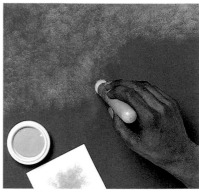

2 *Pour mint-green paint into a dish. Dip a short stipple brush into the paint, dab off almost all of it on a piece of paper towel, then jab lightly at the container surface for a speckled effect.*

3 *Select a light blue-green paint, and pour it into a clean dish. Repeat the stippling process with a clean brush, but work over different areas of the surface to create random concentrations of color. If you are not pleased with the effect, simply reapply the olive-green paint, and start the stippling process again.*

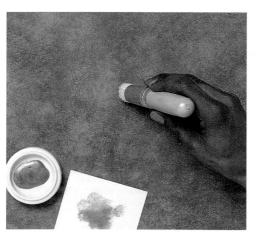

4 *To add the finishing touches to the verdigris effect, use a clean stipple brush to apply a little bronze gilt cream, highlighting any edges, corners, or raised moldings on the container. Gilt cream dries instantly, so apply it sparingly. Alternatively, spread a thin layer of cream on the palm of your hand, and smear it lightly and randomly over the surface of the container.*

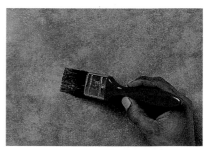

5 *Protect the container against the weather with a coat of clear, matte, waterproof varnish (see p. 105). Apply with a clean paint brush, and allow to dry. Repeat twice.*

APPLYING A CRACKLEGLAZE PAINT FINISH

1 To achieve a striking crackleglaze paint finish that will give your container an aged appearance, apply a base coat of gold acrylic paint to a clean and appropriately primed surface.

2 When the paint is dry, use a clean brush to apply a coat of commercial crackleglaze. For the most successful finish, apply the glaze horizontally, in one direction only, and in a single stroke.

3 Once the glaze is dry, apply a coat of acrylic paint in a second color of your choice, turning the container onto its side and working at a right angle to the previous strokes. Apply the paint with a single stroke of the brush.

4 To speed up the drying process and increase the size of the cracks, blow-dry the painted area with a hairdryer. When the surface is dry, seal it against moisture with three coats of an oil-based varnish (see p. 105).

DECORATING A CONTAINER WITH MOSAIC TILES

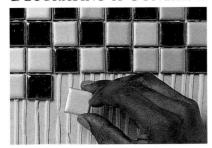

1 Arrange the tiles in your chosen pattern on a flat surface. Apply waterproof tile adhesive in ⅛-in (3-mm) stripes over one side of the container, then lay one row of tiles at a time, leaving ⅛ in (3 mm) between each tile.

2 Wipe off any excess adhesive from the surface of the tiles with a damp cloth, then allow to dry. Fill the gaps between the tiles with ready-mixed waterproof grout, pressing it firmly into the cracks with a small sponge.

3 While the grout is still wet, carefully wipe off any excess with a clean, damp cloth, polishing the tiles at the same time. For a neat finish, run the end of a matchstick over the grout.

LAYING LARGE TILES

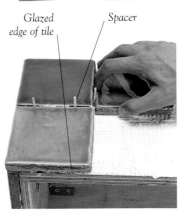

Glazed edge of tile   Spacer

Measure the container to determine how many tiles you need. If they do not align, use a tile cutter to cut tiles to fit. Apply adhesive (see Step 1, left), then position each tile, using spacers to separate them. Ensure that the glazed sides of a tile are showing at each edge and corner. After 12 hours, remove the spacers, and grout (see Steps 2 and 3, left).

LOOKING AFTER CONTAINERS

A planted-up container requires the minimum of care, but circumstances may make it necessary to protect the pot. A terracotta container that is exposed to severe cold will benefit from insulation. If you decide instead to move a planted-up pot to a sheltered place in winter, assess the weight of the container before selecting a method of removal. You may also have to secure a container if it is vulnerable to theft.

MENDING A CRACK

Twist ends tightly

A minor crack in a terracotta pot can be mended with garden wire. Firmly wrap the wire twice around the pot, just below the rim, and twist the ends to secure it. A pot with large cracks is beyond repair. Use the pieces for crocking (see p. 112).

MOVING CONTAINERS

Pull burlap slowly

DRAGGING A POT

If a container is too heavy to carry, drag it onto a burlap bag or piece of carpet, then maneuver the container into position by pulling the burlap or carpet toward you. Secure vulnerable or potentially harmful foliage, such as holly, before moving the plant.

Vulnerable leaves tied with garden twine

Delicate branches are unlikely to be damaged by this method of removal

Trolley strap threaded through handle on container

Incline trolley at 45-degree angle to move weight easily

WHEELING A CONTAINER

Use a sturdy folding luggage trolley to move an unwieldy container over long distances or up steps. Secure the container using the trolley straps. Alternatively, use a skateboard for moving a large container over a short distance on level ground.

SECURING CONTAINERS

Chain wound twice around railing

Padlock secures chain

USING A LOCK AND CHAIN

A container positioned at the front of a building may tempt thieves. To prevent theft, thread a sturdy length of chain through the drainage hole of the container before planting it up. Wrap the chain around a nearby railing or post, and secure the ends with a padlock.

Bricks cover base of container

PLANTING UP WITH BRICKS

If you are unable to chain up a container, consider preventing theft by making the pot too heavy to move. Put the container in position first, since you will not be able to move it once it is planted. Cover the bottom with a layer of broken bricks or rubble, then plant up.

OVERWINTERING A PLANTED-UP CONTAINER

Vulnerable containers, such as those made from terracotta, and tender plants must be protected through the winter to avoid frost and cold damage. If a planted-up container is too heavy to move or you do not have room for it indoors, it will need to be insulated.

1 With a spiky plant, such as *Yucca filamentosa*, gather up the foliage, and tie it loosely with soft garden twine.

Hold leaves of plant gently but firmly

2 Wrap the foliage with garden fleece, ensuring that the plant is completely covered, and secure the fleece with staples or pins. In an emergency, a net curtain will protect foliage from overnight frost.

Staple fleece in place

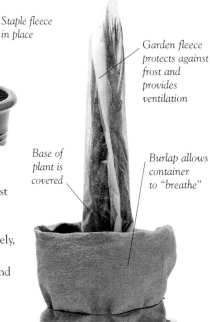

Garden fleece protects against frost and provides ventilation

Base of plant is covered

Burlap allows container to "breathe"

3 Protect the terracotta pot against frost by wrapping a burlap bag around the pot and tying the bag in place with garden twine. Alternatively, use bubble plastic, several layers of newspaper, or even an old coat. Stand the pot on a piece of polystyrene to prevent damage from ground frost.

Polystyrene insulates pot against cold ground

SELECTING HEALTHY PLANTS

When you garden in a container, every plant that you grow is on display and will need to be kept in peak condition. For the best results, make sure that you select the healthiest specimens available. Whether choosing a bulb, a container-grown plant that has been raised in its pot, or a bare-root plant that is sold with its roots clean of soil, check that the plant has been well tended and is free from pests and diseases. A containerized plant with roots growing out of the bottom of its pot, or with weeds and moss on the soil mix, has remained too long in its pot and should be avoided.

CHOOSING A BULB

A healthy bulb (or a corm or tuber) feels firm and plump, and its growing tip and tunic – the brown, outer skin – are intact. Avoid specimens that look shrivelled, have traces of green mold, or are soft to the touch. Store in cool, dry conditions before planting.

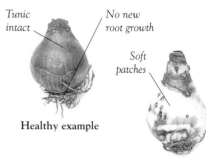

Tunic intact

No new root growth

Soft patches

Healthy example

Poor example

CHOOSING A SHRUB

Select the bushiest shrub, rather than the tallest. Look for vigorous growth at the base of the plant, and slide the pot off the rootball to check that the specimen has a well-established root system.

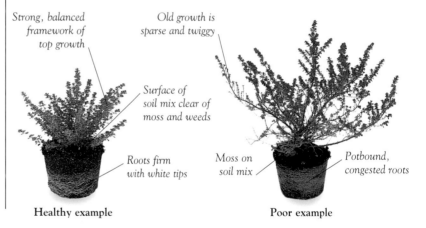

Strong, balanced framework of top growth

Old growth is sparse and twiggy

Surface of soil mix clear of moss and weeds

Roots firm with white tips

Moss on soil mix

Potbound, congested roots

Healthy example

Poor example

CHOOSING A ROSE

Buy a bare-root rose only if you can plant it immediately. When selecting a container-grown rose in leaf, ensure that it is not a bare-root rose that has been potted recently, since it may suffer when you plant it. To check, lift the rose by its main shoot. If it moves within the pot, it has not been container-grown. Avoid plants that have thin shoots or distorted growth.

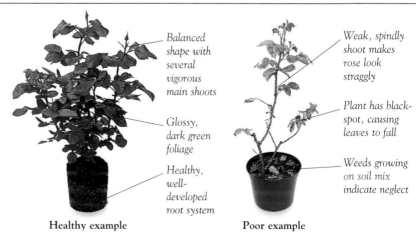

Balanced shape with several vigorous main shoots

Glossy, dark green foliage

Healthy, well-developed root system

Weak, spindly shoot makes rose look straggly

Plant has black-spot, causing leaves to fall

Weeds growing on soil mix indicate neglect

Healthy example

Poor example

CHOOSING A PERENNIAL

Select a perennial that has healthy, vigorous foliage. When buying in spring, look for strong, new growth at the base of the plant. Varieties that die back in winter often look tired at the end of a summer in a garden center and are sold at reduced prices. These specimens are worth buying, since they will produce healthy new growth in spring. Plant them as soon as possible.

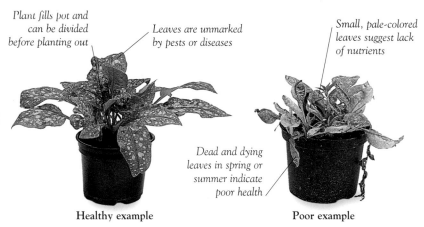

Plant fills pot and can be divided before planting out

Leaves are unmarked by pests or diseases

Small, pale-colored leaves suggest lack of nutrients

Dead and dying leaves in spring or summer indicate poor health

Healthy example

Poor example

CHOOSING AN ANNUAL

Annuals are used to provide instant color, so it is tempting to choose plants that are already covered with flowers. It is best, however, to buy specimens with a large number of buds, since these will produce a succession of flowers. Select sturdy, bushy plants, avoiding those that are drawn and leggy. Check foliage for signs of gray mold and rot. Tender and marginally hardy annuals are often put out for sale before it is wise to plant them outdoors, so avoid buying these plants until frost danger has passed.

Plenty of buds for future flowers

Healthy, green foliage

Dense, bushy growth

Healthy example

Uneven, straggly growth

Diseased leaves

Poor example

CHOOSING A TRAY OF ANNUALS

Weak, spindly growth

Diseased leaves have fungal growth

Dead and dying foliage suggests neglect

Poor example

Save money by buying annual bedding plants in a tray, rather than in pots. Ensure that the plants are bushy, with healthy green foliage and plenty of buds, so that they will establish well when planted. Avoid any specimens that are leggy, have dead or dying leaves, or look like they have been in the box too long. Check that roots are not growing out of the drainage holes at the bottom of the box.

PREPARING FOR PLANTING

One of the joys of container gardening is that you need little in the way of tools and equipment to plant up and maintain your display. It is even possible to improvise with everyday household implements if your budget is limited. However, a good hand trowel and watering can are worth acquiring, since these are the items you will need most frequently. Always clean tools after use, and store out of the reach of children.

PLANTING AND DRAINAGE MATERIALS

Place terracotta crocks or polystyrene pieces in the bottom of a container to aid drainage. For permanent plantings – shrubs, trees, and climbers – use a soil-based potting mix; for hanging baskets, a light, soil-less type. Add water-retaining granules to conserve water. Mix in gravel for free-draining soil mix.

Terracotta crocks   Polystyrene pieces

Water-retaining granules   Potting mix   Gravel

HAND TOOLS

Buy good-quality tools made of stainless or forged steel, since these will perform efficiently, not rust, and be cost-effective. Ensure that all tools, especially the fork and trowel, are comfortable to hold. To prolong their working life, wipe tools with an oily rag after use, and have cutting implements, such as pruners and shears, sharpened regularly.

Safety catch secures sharp blades

Fork   Trowel   Pruners   Shears

IMPROVISED TOOL KIT

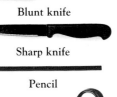

Fork

Blunt knife

Sharp knife

Pencil

Scissors

If you are looking after only a limited number of containers, try improvising your tool kit. Use an old fork as a hand fork, a sharp knife or scissors for pruning, and a pencil or blunt knife for sowing seeds and planting small bulbs.

WATERING EQUIPMENT

Frequent, regular, and generous watering is vital to the successful growth of most container plants, so it is important that your watering tools are appropriate for carrying out this task. If you are looking after only a few plants in windowboxes or small pots, a watering can will be sufficient. For a large group of containers, you will need a hose and possibly one or two attachments.

WATERING CAN

Choose a lightweight watering can that is well balanced and comfortable to hold when full. Use a rose nozzle when applying liquid fertilizer to leaves.

HOSE AND ATTACHMENTS

Use a spray gun attached to a hose to save time when watering a large number of containers. Foliage can act as an umbrella so make sure that the soil mix is thoroughly soaked. Use a lance attached to a hose to reach hanging baskets.

Adjustable nozzle controls force of water

Spray gun

Lever triggers water flow

Attachments can be fitted to hose

Wide opening for easy filling

Hose

Rose nozzle

End of hose connects to tap

Watering can

End of lance is curved to reach soil mix in hanging baskets

Lance

A MICRO-IRRIGATION SYSTEM FOR A CONTAINER GARDEN

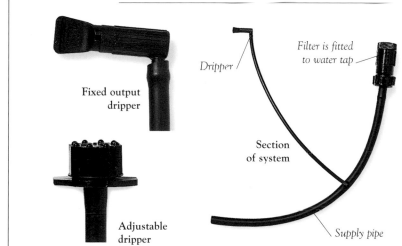

Fixed output dripper

Adjustable dripper

Dripper

Section of system

Filter is fitted to water tap

Supply pipe

A simple micro-irrigation system connected to a tap is ideal for the efficient watering of a large number of plants in containers. Fitted with tiny drippers or sprinklers, this type of system will allow you to control the amount of water discharged to the plants. Fixed output drippers are suitable for most situations, but more sophisticated, adjustable attachments are also available. Place one dripper at the base of each plant to ensure that the water goes directly to the roots. Install a timer to ensure that your plants are watered in your absence.

PLANTING BULBS & SHRUBS

It is worth making sure that planted-up containers look attractive for the longest period of time, particularly if they are your only garden. The best way to achieve this is by growing combinations of shrubs, perennials, annuals, and bulbs. Use evergreens to provide interest and color through the year, and add other plants that peak at different times. In a mixed display, plant the permanent subjects first in soil mix that suits their needs, then fill in around them with any temporary additions.

CREATING AN ARRANGEMENT WITH BULBS

Plant spring-flowering bulbs as soon as possible after purchase, from mid-autumn to early winter – check the packaging for individual planting times. Create an impressive display by planting the bulbs in layers. Include long-flowering pansies and evergreen ivy to provide interest during autumn and winter, while the bulbs are growing.

YOU WILL NEED:

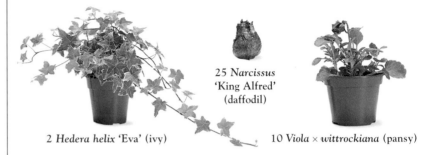

25 *Narcissus* 'King Alfred' (daffodil)

2 *Hedera helix* 'Eva' (ivy)

10 *Viola* × *wittrockiana* (pansy)

PLANTING IN LAYERS

Scatter crocks in the bottom of a pot, and cover with soil mix. Add a layer of bulbs, pointed ends up, and cover with 3 in (8 cm) of soil mix. Add two more layers of bulbs, giving the pot an eighth of a turn between each. Cover with soil mix so that the tips of the top layer of bulbs just show, and position the plants between them. Fill with soil mix to ¾ in (2 cm) below the rim. Water.

UNPOTTING A PLANT

Support crown of plant with fingers

To remove a plant from its pot, place the crown between your middle and index fingers, tip up the pot, and strike the base with the heel of your other hand. Gently pull the container off the rootball.

Ivy planted around edge of pot so stems will fall over rim

Tips of top layer of daffodils just protrude through soil mix

Pot given eighth of a turn between bulb layers, to give shoots room to grow

Terracotta crocks cover bottom of pot to help drainage

Pansies
provide
winter
color

Trailing ivy
adds shape

WINTER GROWTH
Throughout mild winters, the pansies
are in flower, and the ivy trails
attractively over the rim. Remove all
dead flowers to encourage new blooms.

Daffodils grow
to 12 in
(30 cm) tall

Ivy has been
thinned to
encourage
bushy growth

SPRING COLOR
By midspring, the arrangement is at its best – the
daffodils are in flower, along with the pansies, and the
ivy has produced new leaves. Give it a weak liquid feed
every week or so, as the daffodil foliage begins to die.

PLANTING A LARGE SHRUB IN A NEW CONTAINER

Line base
of pot with
polystyrene

1 To provide
drainage for a
shrub, put a 4-in
(10-cm) layer of
polystyrene pieces or
terracotta crocks in
the bottom of a pot,
making sure that the
drainage hole is not
blocked. Fill the pot
to about one-third
full of soil mix.

2 To ensure that the
shrub is planted at
the right level, place
it, still in its pot, in
the new container.
Add or remove soil
mix to leave the top
of the rootball
1½ in (4 cm) below
the rim. Remove the
shrub from its pot (see
opposite) and, if the
roots are congested,
gently tease them out.

Hold plant
at base of
stem

3 Place the shrub in
the center of the
new container. Pack
fresh soil mix around
the shrub until the
soil is at the same
level as the rootball
and 1½ in (4 cm)
below the rim of
the pot. Firm the soil
mix well with your
fist to eliminate air
pockets, and top up
if necessary. Water
the shrub thoroughly
after planting.

PLANTING UP BOXES & BASKETS

A windowledge, small patio, or a wall from which a basket can be hung provides a welcome opportunity to enjoy the pleasures of gardening, and also to experiment with unusual containers. If an arrangement does not provide year-round interest, consider using temporary methods to add seasonal color, such as plunging pots into an existing planting. In practical terms, it is important to make sure that a windowbox or the bracket for a hanging basket is securely attached in position, since containers are heavy when filled with damp soil mix and plants.

PLANTING UP A WINDOWBOX

1 *Ensure that there is adequate drainage in the base of the window-box, making new holes if necessary (see p. 105). Add a layer of crocks, then half-fill the box with soil mix.*

2 *Experiment with the positions of the potted plants until you are happy with the display. Place tall plants at the back of the box and trailing plants at the sides and front.*

Support plant at crown

3 *When all the plants are positioned, remove them from their pots (see p. 114). Gently tease out the roots, and place each plant in a shallow depression in the soil mix.*

Use fingertips to firm soil

4 *Fill the box with fresh soil mix to a level ¾ in (2 cm) below the rim, firming well around each plant. Water thoroughly, and fill any hollows that appear with extra soil mix.*

MAKING A TEMPORARY DISPLAY IN A WINDOWBOX

Place new liner in box for instant display

Seasonal method

If you have space, create a year-round display in a windowbox by planting arrangements for different seasons in separate plastic liners. Keep a planted-up liner in a sheltered area, giving the plants time to become established before replacing the previous season's display.

Plunge method

Add temporary interest to a permanent design by plunging plants into the soil mix without removing them from their pots. In this way, summer- and winter-flowering annuals and perennials can be replaced without disturbing the main arrangement.

PREPARING A HANGING BASKET

Cut slit
with scissors

Ease rootball
into place

Trim
overlap
to 2 in
(5 cm)

1 Balance the basket on a bucket and fit it with a liner, trimming interior overlaps to fit. Use a coir liner – it is easy to handle and, unlike moss, can be used again.

2 To achieve a "ball of flowers" effect with trailing plants, cut slits at varying levels in the sides of the liner. Fill the basket with soil mix to just below the level of the lowest cut.

3 Moisten the rootball of a trailing plant. Squeeze it gently to form a sausage shape, then carefully push it through a slit. Repeat. Cover each rootball with fresh soil mix.

Position large
plant in center

4 Arrange the remaining potted plants on top of the soil mix, adjusting the display to your liking. Carefully remove each plant from its pot (see p. 114), and place in the basket.

5 Fill gaps between the plants with soil mix, firming well. Trim the top of the liner, leaving ¾ in (2 cm) above the basket's rim to allow space for watering.

USING A WICKER BASKET AS A CONTAINER

1 Paint the interior and exterior of the basket with three coats of varnish or wood preservative. Allow to dry. Arrange plastic pots upside down on the base to assist drainage.

2 Line the basket with a thick black plastic sheet, leaving a generous overlap at the top. Cut a few 1-in (2.5-cm) slits in the bottom of the lining to provide drainage.

3 Plant up the basket, then trim off the excess plastic to about 2 in (5 cm) over the top of the basket. Tuck the remainder of the plastic into the basket, out of sight.

MAINTAINING PLANTS

Plants in pots are entirely dependent on you for their food and water. The key to successful container gardening is to ensure that they are supplied with adequate amounts of both. Remember that the needs of a plant will vary according to the weather and the seasons. A small container should be watered at least once a day in hot weather, and even in rain, since the heaviest downpour cannot provide soil mix with sufficient moisture for a plant's requirements.

WATERING PLANTS EFFECTIVELY

To moisten soil mix thoroughly, drench the container until water runs out through the drainage holes at the bottom of the pot, and the pot feels heavy when lifted. If soil mix is very dry, water can run down the sides and out of the bottom without wetting the soil mix at all.

REVIVING A DRIED-OUT PLANT

Fill a bowl or sink with tepid water, then immerse the dried-out plant in its pot so that the rim of the pot is just below the surface of the water. When air bubbles no longer appear, remove the container from the water.

Push pot under water

Water slowly to prevent splashing and loss of soil mix

Space between soil mix and rim of pot should be filled with water

USING A WATERING CAN

The foliage and flowers of a plant can act as an umbrella, preventing water from reaching the soil mix and depriving the roots of moisture. Water soil mix directly at a plant's base – where it will be of most benefit – by using a watering can without a rose nozzle.

Pulley system allows basket to be raised and lowered

USING A PULLEY

Stretching up to water a hanging basket is tiring and awkward. Hang a basket on a bracket with a pulley system so that it can be lowered to a convenient height. Stop watering when water trickles through the liner.

Keep water running at slow trickle for effective watering

USING A LANCE

If a basket is hanging at a fixed height, water it using a lance (see p. 113) attached to a hose. Squeeze the lance's trigger gently to prevent soil mix and water from splashing over the edge.

Aim point of lance directly at soil mix

Away-from-home Watering

Fabric transports water from bucket to soil mix

Capillary matting

Tray is filled with water before plants are positioned

Improvising a Self-watering System
Create a homemade, self-watering system by standing a bucket of water on a support, raising it above the container. Weight one end of a strip of absorbent fabric at the bottom of the bucket, and push the other end into the soil mix.

Using Capillary Matting
Cover the base of two trays with a strip of capillary matting. Stand the containers in one tray, and fill the other with water. The matting will remain wet, allowing the plants to take up moisture through the drainage holes of their pots.

Cleaning Evergreen Leaves

Support back of leaf with hand

Dust and pollution not only spoil the appearance of a plant, they also prevent it from absorbing essential gases and sunlight. Evergreen leaves are particularly affected, since they live for a number of years. Wipe regularly with a damp cloth or sponge to remove layers of grime.

Feeding Plants in Containers
After approximately one month, the plants in a container have absorbed all the nutrients available in the soil mix and will need regular additional feeding. Whichever type of fertilizer you choose, do not apply more than the recommended amount, since an excess of fertilizer is likely to damage a plant.

Soluble fertilizer

Liquid fertilizer

Controlled-release fertilizer plugs

Using Fertilizer
Apply a general fertilizer in a soluble form, or use liquid fertilizer to encourage free flowering through the season. Alternatively, push a controlled-release fertilizer plug into the soil mix near the base of a plant at the beginning of the growing season. The plug will release nutrients for about six months. Always follow the manufacturer's instructions.

Use an old fork to remove soil mix

Top-dressing a Plant
Give a boost to a tired-looking shrub or perennial by removing the top 2 in (5 cm) of its soil mix every year or two. Fill with a layer of fresh soil mix plus controlled-release fertilizer, and water well.

REPOTTING & TRIMMING

A potted plant will outgrow its container eventually, which may result in the plant looking tired and failing to grow as vigorously as before. To confirm that a plant needs repotting, carefully remove it from its pot, and examine the roots. If they are very congested, transfer the plant to a larger container. Keep a plant looking healthy and attractive with regular trimming and deadheading to encourage the growth of new foliage and flowers. Trimming also has a decorative function – use pruners to create different types of topiary.

REPOTTING A PLANT

1 Check that the new pot is the correct size by slipping the plant – still in its old pot – inside it. An all-around gap of about 1 in (2.5 cm) between the sides of the two pots is ideal.

Check new pot is large enough before repotting

2 Soak the rootball of the plant while it is still in its original container to reduce the impact of the move, and to help establish it in its new soil mix.

Support plant by holding crown between your fingers

3 Loosened roots will quickly grow out into the new soil mix, so carefully tease out congested roots and, using a sharp knife, trim any that are damaged or dead. Check the rootball for signs of pests, such as mealybug, and remove any that you find.

Fill pot with soil mix to within 1 in (2.5 cm) of rim

4 Place a layer of crocks on the bottom of the new pot, and cover with soil mix. Firm down, then position the plant on top. Fill around the rootball with fresh soil mix, firming it with your fingers to remove air pockets.

Prune plant with sharp scissors to encourage new growth

5 Trim off any dead leaves and straggly or damaged stems, add a controlled-release fertilizer plug (see p. 119), and water the soil mix thoroughly.

REMOVING CACTI FROM THEIR CONTAINERS

HANDLING WITH A STRIP OF PAPER
Cacti spines are sharp, so take care when handling them. Fast-growing cacti need repotting every 2–3 years. To remove a small cactus, wrap a strip of folded paper around it, and gently pull it out of the pot.

HANDLING WITH A GLOVE
To remove a delicate cactus from its pot, put on a pair of very sturdy gardening gloves to avoid being pricked by the spines. Tip the container up with one hand, and ease the plant into your other hand.

TRAINING AN IVY PYRAMID

1 In order to encourage new growth and achieve dense cover over a wire topiary frame, weave the ivy shoots laterally around the frame so that the production of side shoots is stimulated.

2 As the ivy grows, continue to wrap it around the frame. When it has covered the frame completely, pinch out the growing tip on each stem to ensure that the plant remains small and bushy.

TRIMMING A TOPIARY

CLIPPING A BOXWOOD GLOBE
Trim a rounded topiary shape in boxwood using a pair of pruners. Stand back frequently to check that the overall shape is being preserved.

DEADHEADING FLOWERING ANNUALS

REMOVING LARGE FLOWERS
Pinch off dead flowers and their seed capsules between your thumb and forefinger, encouraging the plant to flower prolifically.

REMOVING SMALL FLOWERS
Some flowers are too small to remove individually, so trim back faded stems with scissors to neaten the plant and stimulate new growth.

DEADHEADING A ROSE

REMOVING A CLUSTER
To encourage new flowering shoots and prevent the tips of shoots from dying, prune faded clusters of flowers back to the first outward-facing leaf.

PROPAGATING PLANTS

Once you have experienced the pleasure of successfully growing plants in containers, you may want to take up the exciting challenge of growing new plants. Even if a window-ledge is the only growing space available, it is still possible to take cuttings from tender perennials, such as fuchsias and geraniums, and to grow plants from seed. Many herbaceous plants are propagated by division and can be instantly planted into new containers. If you are unable to protect mature, tender plants during winter, use these methods to replace them the following summer.

TAKING A CUTTING

Handle knife carefully to avoid damaging plant

Cut leaf stem where it joins main stalk

1 Choose a healthy, young shoot that has not yet flowered. With a sharp knife, cut straight across the chosen stem, below the third leaf joint down from the growing tip.

2 Place the cutting on a flat surface. Reduce excess water loss through the leaf pores by removing all but the top few leaves. Pinch out any flower buds that may have formed.

3 Trim the base of the cutting to just below the lowest leaf joint, making a straight, clean cut. Take care not to leave any jagged edges, since these could cause the cutting to rot. Dip the newly cut end into hormone rooting powder.

GROWING A CUTTING IN WATER

Cuttings of some plants, such as impatiens, tradescantias, and begonias, will quickly produce roots in water. Take a cutting approximately 4 in (10 cm) long, and strip off all but the top few leaves. Place it in a small jar of water, using the rim to keep its leaves clear of the water. When ¼–1½ in (2–4 cm) of root has formed, plant in soil mix.

4 Moisten and firm the soil mix in a small pot, make a hole in the mix with a pencil or dibber, and insert the cutting. Put the pot in a warm, light place out of direct sun. Water from below by standing the pot in a tray or saucer filled with water.

Insert cutting in hole 1 in (2.5 cm) deep

GROWING PLANTS FROM SEED

1 *In a pot or seed tray, spread a thin layer of gravel, then fill almost to the rim with seed soil mix. Firm lightly, and water from below. Sow the seed very thinly onto the surface, then cover lightly with more mix.*

Scatter seed evenly over surface

2 *Cover the pot or tray with a piece of clear, thin plastic, ensuring that the plastic is pulled tight. Put the pot in a light place, out of direct sun, where a steady, warm temperature is maintained.*

Stretch plastic tight to seal in moisture

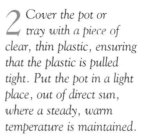

3 *When the seeds have germinated and are large enough to handle, use an old fork to lift out a small clump of seedlings. Tease them apart carefully, without damaging their roots.*

4 *Fill a pot with soil mix. Hold each seedling by a leaf – do not risk damaging the root system by touching any of the roots – and plant it in a hole 1 in (2.5 cm) deep and 1½ in (4 cm) away from other seedlings. Gently firm the soil mix and water from below.*

DIVIDING A HERBACEOUS PLANT

1 *When a herbaceous plant outgrows its pot, it can be split into several new plants. To remove the plant from its pot, support the crown between your fingers, strike the base, and ease out the rootball.*

2 *Gently brush away any excess soil mix surrounding the rootball, enabling you to see clearly the separate sections of the root system. Be careful to avoid unnecessary damage to the roots, since this will inhibit new growth.*

3 *Inspect the rootball to establish where it naturally divides. Carefully push your thumbs into the rootball at this point, and slowly lever it apart. To divide a tough plant, use a sharp knife, and cut the rootball into sections.*

Use thumbs to lever rootball apart

4 *Plant up the divisions in individual pots filled with soil mix. Water in, and continue to water regularly. New growth indicates that their roots have become established in the soil mix. Feed with liquid fertilizer four to six weeks after replanting.*

Firm down soil mix around plant

CONTROLLING PROBLEMS

Plants can be seriously damaged by neglect as well as by pests and diseases. Make them resistant to attack by keeping them healthy, and regularly check the plants over when you water. Use this chart to examine a plant, identify a particular problem, and take immediate, appropriate action. Moving from general to specific problems, this chart will help you to maintain a healthy display.

PLANT PROBLEMS	SYMPTOMS AND CAUSES	CONTROLS
DISCOLORED LEAVES	The discoloration of leaves is a general and common problem that may be caused by pests such as aphids or spider mites, molds such as powdery mildew, viral diseases, drought, sun- or wind-scorch, or nutrient deficiency.	Carefully examine the fronts and backs of the leaves of the plant, its stems, and – if necessary – its base and roots. Use the descriptions on this page and opposite to determine the specific cause of the problem, and take action promptly.
POTBOUND ROOTS	A plant's growth can be slowed by its roots becoming potbound. This is caused by the plant outgrowing its container. The roots form a tangled circle around the soil mix, preventing the absorption of food and water.	Tease the roots out carefully from around the rootball, and trim off the longest. Replant in a larger pot in fresh soil mix, and feed and water well. Check the root system regularly, and repot when necessary.
EATEN PETALS AND LEAVES	Holes in flowers and foliage and the complete removal of leaves are caused by a range of pests, including slugs and snails, earwigs, lily beetles, flea beetles, caterpillars, leaf-cutting bees, sowbugs, and vine weevils.	Pick pests off by hand in the early stages of an attack, or spray with a fine water jet to remove them. Use a suitable chemical pesticide to control a persistent problem, and always follow the manufacturer's instructions.
POWDERY MILDEW	White, powdery fungus can affect many types of plant, leading to foliage turning yellow and falling. It appears on the upper surfaces of leaves and on flowers, stems, and fruits. It is usually brought on by overly dry soil.	Pick off affected growth immediately. If the mildew persists, spray with a suitable fungicide. Mulch around affected plants, and make sure that they are never overly dry at the roots. Avoid watering from above.
BLACK-SPOT	This disease is caused by fungus and appears on rose leaves in warm, wet weather in the form of black spots, which may merge into patches. Affected leaves turn yellow and die – a sustained attack can defoliate a plant.	Remove diseased leaves at the first sign of infection, and spray the whole plant with fungicide. Avoid splashing the leaves with water. If blackspot is persistent, replace the rose with a variety bred for disease resistance.

PLANT PROBLEMS	SYMPTOMS AND CAUSES	CONTROLS
RING SPOTS	Discoloration in a ring pattern is a symptom, along with mottling and streaking of foliage, of several viral diseases that can affect many types of plant. Some are transmitted by pests, such as aphids; others are seed-borne.	Viral diseases cannot be cured. Remove and discard an affected plant immediately, and clean its container with diluted disinfectant. Buy a certified virus-free plant to replace it, and plant in fresh soil mix.
MAGNESIUM DEFICIENCY	Yellow discoloration between leaf veins on mainly acid-loving plants is usually the result of magnesium deficiency, which may be caused by overfeeding with potash.	Water the soil mix thoroughly, and spray the leaves with magnesium sulfate or a fertilizer for acid-loving plants. Replant in spring or summer in fresh, acidic soil mix.
WILTING	Wilted leaves are a symptom of drought. Starting with the lower part of a plant, this condition moves upward, often causing leaves to then fall. Untreated, it will lead to the collapse, defoliation, and death of a plant.	If the majority of the plant's foliage remains green, it may be revived. Water thoroughly until the pot feels noticeably heavier, or immerse the container in water until air bubbles no longer appear on the surface.
APHIDS	Thick infestations of sap-sucking aphids on stems, buds, and leaves weaken growth, distort shoots and flowers, cover foliage in sticky honeydew, and support the growth of sooty mold.	Remove small colonies of aphids from a plant by rubbing them off with your fingers. Alternatively, spray them with a jet of water and liquid detergent, or apply a suitable pesticide.
SPIDER MITES	A fine, silky webbing covering a plant indicates the presence of spider mites. They may be found on the undersides of leaves that have become dull with fine, yellow-brown mottling. The leaves may eventually die and fall.	Spray the entire plant with pesticide, or use an insecticidal liquid soap. Some strains are resistant to chemical controls. Try introducing the predatory mite *Phytoseiulus persimilis*, which will eat the spider mites.
SPITBUGS	Frothy white blobs on plants in early summer conceal the young nymphs of insects called leaf hoppers. These pests suck a plant's sap and distort young growth but do little serious damage.	Treatment is not always necessary for these pests. However, if you wish to remove them, pick the nymphs off by hand, or spray gently with water, using the finest jet setting on a hand sprayer.
VINE WEEVILS	From late summer to spring, fat, white weevil grubs can gnaw through a plant's roots, causing the plant to collapse and die. Adult beetles eat the leaves of shrubs and perennials at night.	Biological control is the only effective way to remove these pests. In summer, water the soil mix with a treatment containing parasitic nematodes. The nematodes will kill the grubs.

PLANTER'S GUIDE

FABULOUS FOLIAGE
While flowers usually produce the
brightest color in an arrangement,
foliage can be used to great effect
for shape, texture, and color.

Choosing a planting is the most exciting aspect of
container gardening, since there is a vast range
of plants available. While annuals continue to be popular,
there are many shrubs, climbers, and perennials – including
grasses and ferns – that thrive in containers and create
a vivid display. The *Plant Index* can assist you in making
this choice, giving the characteristics and correct growing
conditions for all the plants that are included in this book.

LIVING COLOR
Prolifically flowering annuals and
tender perennials, such as New
Guinea Hybrid impatiens and
geraniums, create instant color.

PLANT INDEX

PLANT SYMBOLS

These symbols are used to show the ideal growing conditions for each plant listed in the index. USDA and Canadian hardiness zone numbers are given to indicate the hardiness of a plant. In addition, frost tender plants (T) and those that are grown as annuals (A) are pointed out.

LIGHT	SOIL MIX
☼ sun	◖ wet
✸ semi-shade	◗ moist
✹ shade	◊ well drained

A

Abutilon 'Orangeade'
☼ ◊ T
A tender shrub, this has attractive, maple-like leaves and vibrant, deep orange, lantern-like flowers that are produced from summer to autumn.

Acaena 'Blue Haze'
☼ ◊ US Z 7–9 CAN Z 8
This low-growing, evergreen perennial from New Zealand has tiny, steel-gray leaves and spherical, russet flowers from late summer to autumn.

Acaena microphylla
'Kupferteppich'
☼ ◊ US Z 6–8 CAN Z 7
The copper-tinged, mat-forming foliage of this perennial makes it ideal as an underplanting where it will tumble over the edge of the container.

Acanthus mollis (bear's breeches)
☼ ✸ ◗ US Z 7–10 CAN Z 8
This striking perennial is as valuable for its glossy, architectural, semi-evergreen leaves as for its tall spires of prickly, tubular flowers that are produced in summer. It can reach a height of 4 ft (1.2 m).

Acer palmatum var. dissectum
(Japanese maple)
✸ ◊ US Z 6–8 CAN Z 7
The finely divided leaves of this deciduous shrub or small tree add a Japanese feel to an arrangement. Its green leaves turn vivid red in autumn. Its slow-growing, bushy habit makes it well suited to planting in a container. Protect its young foliage from early morning sun.

Adiantum raddianum
(delta maidenhair fern)
✸ ✹ ◖ T
This delicate, semi-evergreen or evergreen fern has very finely divided, pale green leaflets on wiry, almost black, stems. It thrives in moist, neutral, or acidic soil mix and adds interest to a shady spot.

Aeonium arboreum 'Zwartkop'

Aeonium arboreum 'Zwartkop'
(purple rose tree)
☼ ◊ T
A striking succulent, this bears neatly arranged rosettes of fleshy, dark purple leaves on pale brown stems and resembles a miniature tree.

Agave americana 'Variegata'
(century plant)
☼ ◊ T
A large succulent, this has very sharply pointed, sword-like leaves that are blue-green in color with pale yellow edges. For safety, it is best planted at the back of a group.

Ageratum
☼ ✸ ◗ A
This pretty, low-growing annual is covered throughout the summer with small, brush-like flowers in intense shades of blue, pink, or white. Free-flowering varieties include 'Blue Danube' and 'Summer Snow'.

Allium karataviense
☼ ✸ ◗ US Z 5–9 CAN Z 6
An ornamental member of the onion family, this spring-flowering bulb has broad leaves and large, spherical heads of pinkish purple flowers.

Allium schoenoprasum
(chives)

☼ ✳ ◊ US Z 3–9 CAN Z 4 a

In addition to being an invaluable culinary herb, this perennial is an attractive plant with narrow, tubular leaves and small, round, spiky, pinkish mauve flowers.

Aloe variegata
(partridge-breasted aloe)

☼ ◊ T

An architectural succulent, this has pointed, scoop-like leaves that are attractively marked. Its maximum height is around 9 in (23 cm).

Anchusa capensis 'Blue Angel'

☼ ✳ ◊ A

This bushy annual is easy to look after and produces vibrant blue flowers in great profusion.

Anemone blanda 'Atrocaerulea'

✳ ✴ ◊ US Z 4–8 CAN Z 5

A beautiful corm for a semi-shady spot, this produces star-shaped, blue, daisy-like flowers in spring.

Anethum graveolens (dill)

☼ ◊ A

Dill is an attractive herb with feathery foliage and flat heads of mustard-yellow flowers.

Antirrhinum majus
'White Wonder' (snapdragon)

☼ ◊ A

This medium-sized perennial variety of snapdragon produces spires of pure white flowers all summer long, if it is deadheaded regularly.

Anchusa capensis 'Blue Angel'

Aralia elata 'Variegata'
(Japanese angelica tree)

☼ ✳ ◊ US Z 4–9 CAN Z 5

A deciduous tree or large shrub, this is grown for its outstanding foliage but also has billowing heads of white flowers in late summer. Dead growth should be removed in spring.

Argyranthemum frutescens
(marguerite)

☼ ✳ ◊ T

The marguerite is an evergreen perennial that produces masses of daisy-like, white flowers throughout the summer. It thrives in full sun but will tolerate some shade.

Asplenium nidus
(bird's-nest fern)

✳ ✴ ◊ T

The evergreen bird's-nest fern has broad, flat, light-green fronds. It should be taken indoors in winter.

Asplenium scolopendrium
(hart's-tongue fern)

✳ ✴ ◊ US Z 6–8 CAN Z 7

The hart's-tongue fern is evergreen and has many slender, undulating, bright green fronds. It thrives in moist, alkaline soil mix.

B

Bacopa 'Snowflake'

☼ ✳ ◊ T

This tender perennial – usually grown as an annual – forms a carpet of tiny, rounded leaves and white flowers. It survives outside during mild winters.

Ballota pseudodictamnus

☼ ◊ US Z 7–9 CAN Z 8

A lovely foliage plant, this evergreen shrub has rounded, gray-green leaves that are covered in fine, white hairs, giving it a felted appearance. Tiny, pink flowers appear in summer.

Begonia elatior

✳ ◊ T

This variety of begonia has an upright habit with pointed leaves and gives a continuous display of small, double flowers throughout cool summers. It is grown from seed.

Begonia pendula

✳ ◊ T

The trailing, double blooms of this begonia are perfect for use in a hanging basket. 'Illumination' produces attractive, small, pink flowers.

Begonia × tuberhybrida

✳ ◊ T

Tuberous begonias bear large, frilly flowers all summer long. Tubers can be dried and stored over the winter for use the following year. 'Sensation Yellow' has double, yellow flowers; 'Non-stop' produces double flowers that are available in red, pink, yellow, white, and orange.

Berberis thunbergii 'Rose Glow'
☼ ◗ US Z 5–8 CAN Z 6

Grown for its attractive, marbled foliage in burgundy, pink, and cream, this deciduous shrub also produces yellow flowers in spring, which can be removed to encourage new foliage.

Bidens ferulifolia
☼ ✸ ◗ A

This excellent, tender perennial container plant – often grown as an annual – has trailing, fern-like foliage and produces masses of bright gold flowers in summer. Faded blooms can be removed by pinching them out.

Blechnum spicant (hard fern)
✸ ✸ ◗ US Z 5–8 CAN Z 6

An evergreen fern, this has narrow, pointed, leathery fronds with jagged edges. It can withstand drier, colder weather conditions than many other varieties of fern.

Brachycome multifida
(Swan River daisy)
☼ ◗ A

This annual produces masses of golden-eyed, blue daisies throughout the summer. It is also available in pink and white.

Bracteantha bracteata
'Bright Bikini'
(strawflower)
☼ ◗ A

This annual everlasting flower is available in a range of shiny, bright colors and can be dried for an indoor arrangement by hanging upside down in a dry place.

Buxus sempervirens (boxwood)
✸ ✸ ◗ US Z 6–8 CAN Z 7

Dwarf boxwood is evergreen, shade-tolerant, and can be clipped into attractive shapes, making it an invaluable plant for a container in a formal setting. Unclipped, it may produce small flowers in spring.

C

Calendula officinalis (pot marigold)
☼ ◗ A

This is a traditional favorite, producing attractive semi-double or double flowers all summer in shades ranging from cream to deep orange.

Camellia japonica
'Alba Simplex'
✸ ✸ ◗ US Z 7–9 CAN Z 8

This acid-loving shrub produces single, white flowers in spring. Its glossy, evergreen foliage provides interest all year.

Carex comans 'Bronze Form'
☼ ◗ US Z 6–9 CAN Z 7

This evergreen grass has narrow, bronze foliage and small, rusty brown flowers in late summer.

Camellia japonica **'Alba Simplex'**

Centaurea cyanus 'Dwarf Blue'
(cornflower)
☼ ◗ A

Cornflowers are among the easiest annuals to grow from seed. While blue is the most common flower color, purple, red, pink, and white selections are also available.

Chamaerops humilis
(dwarf fan palm)
☼ ◗ US Z 8–10 CAN Z 9

This slow-growing, evergreen palm has delicate, fan-shaped, glossy leaves. In a large container it can reach a height and spread of 5 ft (1.5 m).

Choisya ternata 'Sundance'
(Mexican orange blossom)
☼ ✸ ◗ US Z 7–9 CAN Z 8

The glossy, golden leaves of this evergreen shrub lighten a dull corner. Scented, starry, white flowers are produced in early summer and will sometimes appear again in early autumn.

Clematis campaniflora
☼ ✸ ◗ US Z 5–9 CAN Z 6

From midsummer to autumn, this small-flowered variety of clematis bears nodding, white flowers that are tinged with violet-blue. It should be pruned back hard in early spring.

Clematis flammula
☼ ✸ ◗ US Z 5–9 CAN Z 6

This clematis produces almond-scented, white flowers in late summer and may retain its attractive, small leaves in a mild winter. It can grow up to 15 ft (4.5 m) in height.

Clematis 'Vino'
☼ ❊ ◗ US Z 5–9 CAN Z 6

A large-flowered hybrid with wine-red petals and yellow stamens, this flowers in early summer and again in early autumn. In early spring, the previous season's growth should be reduced by about one-third.

Convolvulus cneorum
☼ ◔ US Z 7–9 CAN Z 8

From early summer to autumn, this lovely shrub produces white flowers that unfurl from tightly rolled, pink buds. Its foliage has a pearly sheen.

Convolvulus sabatius
syn. C. mauritanicus
☼ ◗ T

An excellent trailing plant for a hanging basket, this tender perennial has small leaves and bears open, violet-blue flowers in summer and autumn.

Cordyline australis 'Torbay Dazzler'
(New Zealand cabbage palm)
☼ ❊ ◔ US Z 9–10 CAN Z 9

A striking, architectural plant, this slow-growing evergreen has narrow, sword-like leaves that are striped with bronze, pink, and cream.

Corylus avellana 'Contorta'
(contorted hazel)
☼ ◗ US Z 3–7 CAN Z 4a

The contorted hazel is grown for its twisted stems in winter and catkins in spring. It is covered by broad, green leaves from late spring to late autumn. If a specimen becomes congested, thin out a few branches, and remove any that are damaged.

Crocosmia 'Lucifer'

Cosmos sulphureus
'Ladybird Scarlet'
☼ ◗ A

An attractive annual, this has foliage that resembles the asparagus fern, and deep red, cup-shaped flowers. Other varieties are available in shades from white and yellow to pink and orange.

Crocosmia 'Emily McKenzie'
☼ ◗ US Z 6–9 CAN Z 7

Grown from corms, this plant has erect, sword-like leaves and sprays of large, burnt orange, funnel-shaped blooms in late summer.

Crocosmia 'Lucifer'
☼ ◗ US Z 6–9 CAN Z 7

This variety of crocosmia flowers approximately one month before 'Emily McKenzie' (see above), producing vibrant, eye-catching, scarlet blooms. Corms can be lifted and stored during winter.

Crocus
☼ ◗ US Z 3–8 CAN Z 4a

A winter- and spring-flowering corm, most varieties produce delicate, satiny, fragrant flowers in a range of colors, from white, cream, and yellow to blue and purple.

Cyclamen hederifolium
❊ ◔ US Z 5–9 CAN Z 6

The small flowers of this corm appear in autumn and range in color from deep pink, through mauve, to white. Its oval leaves are distinctively marked with silver patterning. If allowed, this species will self-seed.

D

Dahlia 'Yellow Hammer'
☼ ◗ A

This annual dwarf dahlia produces single yellow flowers from midsummer to autumn. With a height of about 16 in (40 cm), it is well suited to growing in a container. The flowers of this plant are ideal for cutting.

Diascia 'Blackthorn Apricot'
☼ ◗ US Z 8–9 CAN Z 9

This cultivar flowers freely throughout the summer, its petals a delightful shade of soft apricot-peach. It can be propagated by taking cuttings in late summer.

Diascia rigescens
☼ ◗ US Z 7–9 CAN Z 8

This perennial has trailing stems of small, heart-shaped leaves and produces semi-upright spikes of spurred, soft and dark pink flowers throughout the summer.

Diascia vigilis 'Elliott's Variety'
☼ ◗ US Z 7–9 CAN Z 8

A creeping, carpeting form of the species, this cultivar is also one of the hardiest of diascias and produces spikes of clear pink flowers from midsummer to autumn.

E

Eccremocarpus scaber
(Chilean glory flower)
☼ ◑ US Z 8–10 CAN Z 9
An exotic-looking climber with its flame-orange flowers, this will quickly scramble up a support. It should be protected during winter, or replaced when all danger of frost has passed.

Echeveria elegans
☼ ◊ tender below 41°F (7°C)
The rosettes of this fleshy, blue-green succulent produce long, orange stems with small clusters of coral-pink flowers at the tips.

Echeveria hybrid
☼ ◊ tender below 41°F (7°C)
The rosettes of this succulent freely offset to form small plants. Once these have developed roots, they can be removed and planted up individually. Damp conditions may cause the base to rot so should be avoided.

Epimedium × versicolor
'Sulphureum'
✳ ✸ ◑ US Z 5–9 CAN Z 6
This attractive, carpeting perennial has slim stems that support heart-shaped leaves, which take on a reddish tinge in spring. Delicate, yellow flowers appear in spring.

Erythronium 'Pagoda'
(dog's-tooth violet)
✳ ✸ ◑ US Z 4–8 CAN Z 5
This is a woodland tuber that does well in part shade, producing hanging, pale yellow, turk's-cap flowers in late spring.

Eschscholzia californica 'Dali'
(California poppy)
☼ ◊ A
This annual has brilliant scarlet flowers and finely cut, gray-green leaves. It is easily grown from seed.

Euonymus fortunei
'Emerald Gaiety'
✳ ✸ ◑ US Z 4–8 CAN Z 5
This small, bushy, evergreen shrub is ideal in a shady site. The green-and-white variegated leaves of this cultivar are tinged pink in cold weather.

Euonymus fortunei
'Emerald 'n' Gold'
✳ ✸ ◑ US Z 4–8 CAN Z 5
This variety has gold-and-green variegations and will bring light and a feeling of warmth to a dark corner.

Euonymus fortunei
'Gold Tip'
✳ ✸ ◑ US Z 4–8 CAN Z 5
As this cultivar's name suggests, the tips of its leaves are irregularly edged in gold, slowly fading to cream. The spreading cultivar 'Sunspot' has gold splashes in the center of each leaf.

Epimedium × *versicolor* **'Sulphureum'**

Euonymus japonicus 'Macrophyllus'
(Japanese euonymus)
☼ ✸ ◑ US Z 7–9 CAN Z 8
This upright, bushy, evergreen shrub is larger than *Euonymus fortunei* and has oval, dark green leaves.

Euphorbia griffithii
'Fireglow'
☼ ✸ ◑ US Z 4–9 CAN Z 8
An invaluable, bushy perennial, this has slender, green leaves with a brick-red rib, and striking, burnt orange flowerheads in midsummer. It can be propagated by division in spring. The sap is a skin and eye irritant.

F

Fargesia murieliae 'Simba'
(bamboo)
✳ ✸ ◑ US Z 6–9 CAN Z 7
An evergreen bamboo, this attractive variety produces masses of narrow, pointed, light green leaves on slender canes that can reach a height of 15 ft (4.5 m) in a large container.

Fatsia japonica
(Japanese aralia, Japanese fatsia)
✳ ✸ ◑ US Z 8–10 CAN Z 9
This evergreen shrub is a striking plant for a shady site, with its large, glossy, hand-shaped leaves. Billowing clusters of small, white flowers are produced in late autumn.

Felicia amelloides 'Variegata'
(blue marguerite)
☼ ◑ T
This shrub has cream-and-green variegated leaves and produces vivid blue flowers in summer.

Felicia bergeriana
(kingfisher daisy)

☼ ◑ A

A fast-growing annual, this has small, clear blue flowers with gold centers and plain green leaves.

Festuca glauca 'Elijah Blue'
(blue fescue)

☼ ◑ US Z 4–8 CAN Z 5

The needle-like foliage of this densely tufted, evergreen grass is à vibrant shade of gray-blue. It produces tall flower spikes in summer and can be propagated by division in spring.

Fuchsia
☼ ✸ ◑ T

Available in trailing and upright varieties, this shrub bears delicate, pendulous flowers throughout the summer. Choose a compact type for growing in a container, or prune regularly and severely.

G

Gaillardia pulchella 'Red Plume'
(blanket flower, Indian blanket)

☼ ◑ A

This double-flowered annual produces masses of soft, round flowers in rich shades of gold and red from summer through to late autumn. Single-flowered cultivars are also available.

Glechoma hederacea 'Variegata'
(variegated ground ivy)

☼ ✸ ◑ US Z 5–9 CAN Z 6

This trailing evergreen produces long stems with rounded, sage-green-and-cream variegated leaves. It is vigorous and benefits from regular trimming.

Hakonechloa macra 'Aureola'

H

Hakonechloa macra 'Aureola'
☼ ✸ ◑ US Z 4–9 CAN Z 5

This dramatic, dwarf, perennial grass has green-and-gold leaves in spring and summer, fading to red in autumn before turning warm brown as it dies back.

Hedera canariensis 'Gloire de Marengo' (Canary Island ivy)
☼ ✸ ◑ US Z 5–9 CAN Z 6

A striking, large-leaved ivy, this has cream-and-green variegated foliage and purple stems. It is not as hardy as other ivies and benefits from protection from harsh weather conditions.

Hedera helix 'Esther'
(English ivy)

☼ ✸ ◑ US Z 5–9 CAN Z 6

Edged with white, this small-leaved ivy is fast growing and can be used to create an almost instant display.

Hedera helix 'Eva'
(English ivy)

☼ ✸ ◑ US Z 6–9 CAN Z 6

The small leaves of this variety are icy green with creamy white, irregular variegation. It is less hardy than other ivy cultivars.

Hedera helix 'Glacier'
(English ivy)

☼ ✸ ◑ US Z 5–9 CAN Z 6

One of the best cultivars of ivy for planting in a container, this has silver-and-cream variegation on its small, triangular leaves.

Hedera helix 'Goldheart'
(English ivy)

☼ ✸ ◑ US Z 5–9 CAN Z 6

An excellent ivy variety with a vivid gold center to its triangular, dark green leaves, this is ideal for lightening a dark corner. 'Golden Ingot' has irregular variegation and distinctive, pointed leaf lobes.

Hedera helix 'Pittsburgh'
(English ivy)

☼ ✸ ◑ US Z 5–9 CAN Z 6

This small-leaved ivy variety has dark green leaves with a shiny, bronze cast to them, particularly in cold weather.

Helichrysum petiolare
☼ ✸ ◑ US Z 9–10 CAN Z 9

The rounded, felty, silver foliage of this trailing, evergreen shrub is invaluable for softening the edges of a container. 'Aureum' is the large, gold-leaved variety, while 'Microphyllus' has small, silver leaves.

Helictotrichon sempervirens
(blue oat grass)

☼ ◑ US Z 4–9 CAN Z 5

This stately, evergreen, perennial grass has steel-blue leaves and bears sprays of tiny, straw-colored flowers on upright stems in summer. It can reach a height of 4 ft (1.2 m).

Holcus mollis 'Albovariegatus'
(variegated creeping soft grass)
☼ ◑ ◐ US Z 5–9 CAN Z 6
A spreading, evergreen grass, this perennial produces tufts of variegated green-and-white leaves that are at their brightest in spring and autumn, when new growth comes through.

Hosta undulata var. univittata
(plantain lily, funkia)
◑ ● ◐ US Z 3–9 CAN Z 4a
This perennial has wavy, twisted leaves with green-and-white variegation. Spikes of pale mauve flowers are produced in summer.

Hosta ventricosa var. aureomaculata
(plantain lily, funkia)
◑ ● ◐ US Z 3–9 CAN Z 4a
Another hosta that is well suited to growing in a container, this has deeply ribbed, green leaves that are marked with creamy streaks. Gold may also appear on the foliage if the plant receives some direct sun.

Hyacinthus orientalis
'L'Innocence' (hyacinth)
☼ ◑ ◐ US Z 5–9 CAN Z 6
This spring-flowering bulb bears sweetly scented, white flower spikes. Bulbs should be planted in autumn.

Hydrangea macrophylla
'White Wave'
◑ ◐ US Z 6–9 CAN Z 7
In late summer this deciduous shrub produces large clusters of white flowers, which are accentuated by its dark green, pointed leaves.

I

Ilex aquifolium 'Argentea Marginata' (silver-margined holly)
◑ ● ◐ US Z 6–9 CAN Z 7
The glossy, dark green leaves of this holly are broadly edged in cream. If a male tree is growing nearby, this female selection will bear red berries.

Impatiens New Guinea Hybrid
(impatiens)
◑ ◐ A
These flower prolifically all summer long, and prefer some sun. The New Guinea hybrids are excellent container plants, with their patterned foliage providing a strong contrast to the large, brilliantly colored blooms. Flower colors include white, magenta, and orange.

Impatiens 'Super Elfin'
(impatiens)
◑ ● ◐ A
The Super Elfin range of impatiens are compact, free-flowering annuals that are available in many colors. The Accent Series is a low-growing, large-flowered variety; the Tempo Series has a spreading habit and large flowers.

Ilex aquifolium **'Argentea Marginata'**

Imperata cylindrica 'Rubra'
(Japanese blood grass)
☼ ◑ ◐ US Z 7–9 CAN Z 8
As they emerge, the narrow leaves of this striking grass are light green, but they quickly become a translucent blood-red. It also produces fluffy heads of tiny, silvery flowers.

J

Juniperus procumbens 'Nana'
(Bonin Island juniper)
☼ ◐ US Z 5–9 CAN Z 6
This prostrate conifer forms a dense carpet of mid-green foliage. It is a dwarf variety of juniper and will remain small and compact.

K

Kniphofia 'Little Maid'
(red-hot poker, torch lily)
☼ ◐ US Z 5–9 CAN Z 6
This small red-hot poker has narrow, grass-like foliage and neat spikes of creamy yellow flowers in summer.

Kniphofia uvaria
(red-hot poker, torch lily)
☼ ◐ US Z 5–9 CAN Z 6
A tall evergreen species, this has tightly packed, scarlet buds that open to soft orange-yellow spikes.

L

Lantana 'Aloha'
☼ ◐ T
The clusters of tiny flowers produced by this shrub are often of two shades, creating an attractive effect. The entire plant is poisonous and should be handled with care.

Limnanthes douglasii
(poached-egg flower)

☼ ◊ A

This is an easy annual to grow from seed and will self-seed, if allowed. Masses of yellow and white flowers are produced continuously throughout the summer, and they attract bees.

Lobelia pendula

☼ ✺ ◊ A

The trailing plant *Lobelia pendula* is invaluable in a hanging basket, creating a haze of color from summer to early autumn. It is available in many shades, including blue, pink, red, white, and lilac.

Lobelia 'Crystal Palace'

☼ ✺ ◊ A

This compact, bushy variety of lobelia produces intense, blue flowers and dark green, almost bronze, foliage.

Lonicera nitida 'Baggesen's Gold'
(box-leaf honeysuckle)

☼ ✺ ◊ US Z 7–9 CAN Z 8

The foliage of this small-leaved, evergreen shrub is golden-green in full shade, and bright gold when exposed to sunlight. Very small flowers are produced in spring. It can be clipped to create a topiary effect.

Lotus berthelotii
(fire vine, coral gem)

☼ ◊ T

This tender, trailing perennial has silver leaves and, in hot summers, produces exotic, burnt orange flowers that resemble parrots' beaks.

Mimulus luteus

Lysimachia congestiflora
'Outback Sunset'

☼ ✺ ◊ US Z 6–9 CAN Z 7

This perennial has variegated green and pale yellow leaves with a reddish tinge, and produces large, yellow flowers with a red eye in summer.

Lysimachia nummularia
'Aurea' (creeping Jenny)

☼ ✺ ◊ US Z 3–9 CAN Z 4a

The perennial creeping Jenny has golden leaves on long, spreading stems and produces delicate, golden, cup-shaped flowers in summer.

M

Mahonia japonica

✺ ✹ ◊ US Z 6–8 CAN Z 7

A striking, evergreen shrub, this has whorls of jagged leaves and bears spikes of sweetly scented, yellow flowers in late winter and berries in spring.

Mentha suaveolens 'Variegata'
(pineapple mint)

☼ ✺ ◊ US Z 5–9 CAN Z 6

The perennial pineapple mint has coolly variegated white-and-green, richly aromatic leaves. It can be propagated by division.

Mimulus luteus
(monkeyflower)

✺ ◊ US Z 9–10 CAN Z 9

This upright, perennial variety of monkeyflower produces small, bright yellow flowers, sometimes spotted with red, from spring to summer. It is a rampant grower and can reach a height of 1 ft (30 cm).

Mimulus 'Viva'
(monkeyflower)

✺ ◊ A

This perennial – usually grown as an annual – thrives in shade, producing large, yellow flowers with a scarlet blotch on each petal.

Miscanthus sinensis
'Morning Light'

☼ ◊ US Z 5–10 CAN Z 6

This elegant, perennial grass has narrow, curving, green leaves, edged with creamy white, which create a shimmering, silvery effect.

Muscari botryoides 'Album'
(grape hyacinth)

☼ ◊ US Z 3–7 CAN Z 4a

A spring-flowering bulb, this produces clusters of tiny, white, fragrant blooms. It will reach a height of approximately 6 in (15 cm). Bulbs should be planted in autumn.

N

Narcissus 'Jenny' (daffodil)

☼ ◊ US Z 3–7 CAN Z 4a

This dwarf daffodil is ideal for a pot, with a height of about 1 ft (30 cm). Its flowers have white petals and lemon trumpets that fade to cream.

Narcissus 'King Alfred' (daffodil)
☼ ◊ US Z 3–7 CAN Z 4a

This late-flowering daffodil is a tall variety. It should be positioned in a sheltered area to avoid wind damage.

Nemesia 'Joan Wilder'
☼ ◊ US Z 8–10 CAN Z 9

This variety of nemesia is quick to flower, its upright stems producing soft, lavender-blue flowers with small, bright yellow eyes.

Nicotiana 'Havana Appleblossom' (flowering tobacco)
☼ ✺ ◊ A

This dwarf variety has upward-facing, creamy white flowers with brownish pink backs that stay open all day.

Nicotiana 'Lime Green' (flowering tobacco)
☼ ✺ ◊ A

The flowers produced by this dwarf variety have a pleasing scent and are an unusual but attractive color. Like 'Havana Appleblossom' (see above), its height is restricted to 1 ft (30 cm).

Nolana 'Blue Bird'
☼ ◊ A

This perennial, usually grown as an annual, has trailing stems bearing blue flowers with a white eye. It needs full sun for the flowers to open.

O

Ocimum basilicum (basil)
☼ ◊ A

The fleshy, oval leaves of this annual herb are aromatic and full of flavor. It must be grown indoors in winter.

Ophiopogon planiscapus 'Nigrescens'
☼ ✺ ◊ US Z 5–9 CAN Z 6

One of the few plants with black foliage, this evergreen perennial resembles a grass with its narrow, strap-like leaves. Small clusters of mauve flowers appear in summer.

Opuntia lindheimeri (prickly pear)
☼ ◊ tender below 45°F (7°C)

This cactus has striking, rounded, mid-green, fleshy segments that are covered in small, white dots.

Origanum vulgare 'Aureum' (golden marjoram)
☼ ✺ ◊ US Z 4–8 CAN Z 5

This clump-forming, culinary herb is a perennial. Its bright yellow, young leaves have as much flavor as the green-leaved variety.

Osteospermum 'Buttermilk'
☼ ◊ US Z 8–10 CAN Z 9

An evergreen perennial, this variety of osteospermum has soft yellow, daisy-like flowers with pale centers, and is more upright than other varieties.

Ophiopogon planiscapus 'Nigrescens'

P

Pachycereus schottii (whisker cactus)
☼ ◊ tender below 50°F (10°C)

An upright, deeply ribbed cactus, this has small spines along the top of each rib. In summer, it produces pink flowers that open at night.

Parodia graessneri
☼ ◊ tender below 50°F (10°C)

A small, barrel-shaped cactus with marked ribs that are covered in sharp, golden spines, this produces pale yellow-green flowers in spring. It thrives in direct sun.

Pelargonium (geranium)
☼ ◊ T

A trailing balcony geranium, 'Fire Cascade' bears scarlet flowers in great profusion throughout the summer. 'Blizzard Cascade' is pure white. The upright, bushy series 'Cassandra', 'Paintbox', and 'Tiffany' are all available in mixed colors.

Petroselinum crispum var. *neopolitanum* (flat-leaved parsley)
☼ ✺ ◊ US Z 5–9 CAN Z 6

Flat-leaved parsley thrives in semi-shade. Tiny flowers can be removed to encourage growth. This variety of parsley has a more intense flavor than the curly-leaved type.

Petunia 'Brilliant White'
☼ ◊ A

This trailing variety of petunia is free-flowering and weather resistant. It bears pure white flowers.

Petunia 'Fantasy'

☼ ◊ A

These mound-forming petunias
are covered in flowers, ranging in
color from blue, through red, to
white. 'Junior Fantasy' produces
an endless succession of small flowers
in a wide variety of colors.

Petunia 'Purple Wave'

☼ ◊ A

This large-flowered, trailing variety
of petunia is well suited to a hanging
basket or windowbox, with a spread
of up to 4 ft (1.2 m) across.

Petunia 'Red Carpet'

☼ ◊ A

As its name suggests, this variety of
petunia has a compact, spreading
habit, making it ideal for a container.

Petunia 'Vein'

☼ ◊ A

Plants in this series produce flowers
with distinctive, streaked markings.

Phormium tenax 'Bronze Baby'
(New Zealand flax)

☼ ◊ US Z 7–9 CAN Z 8

A dwarf variety of phormium, this
is a striking foliage plant that forms
clumps of narrow, wine-red, evergreen
leaves that curl over at the tips.

Phygelius capensis 'Indian Chief'

☼ ◊ US Z 7–9 CAN Z 8

From summer to autumn, this upright
plant bears dangling, tubular, coral-
pink flowers with warm yellow
throats. Its maximum height is
approximately 2 ft (60 cm).

Polystichum setiferum 'Divisilobum'

Phyllitis scolopendrium
'Cristatum'

❋ ◊ US Z 4–8 CAN Z 5

A variety of the evergreen hart's-
tongue fern, this has mid-green fronds
with wavy edges and crested tips. It
thrives in alkaline soil mix.

Platycerium bifurcatum
(staghorn fern)

❋ ◊ tender below 41°F (5°C)

This fern has forked fronds and an
arching habit, making it ideal for use in
a hanging basket. It should be planted
in soil mix containing leaf mold.

Plectranthus forsteri 'Marginatus'

☼ ❋ ◊ tender below 50°F (10°C)

An attractive foliage plant, this has
broad, pointed leaves edged in cream.
Its habit is initially upright but –
with time – it will trail over the
sides of its container.

Pleioblastus auricomus
(bamboo)

☼ ❋ ◊ US Z 6–9 CAN Z 7

This comparatively small, slow-
growing, evergreen bamboo has
dense, purple-black stems that bear
bright gold leaves striped with green.

Polystichum setiferum
'Divisilobum' (soft shield fern)

❋ ❋ ◊ US Z 6–9 CAN Z 7

This evergreen or semi-evergreen fern
has mid-green, very finely divided,
slender, pointed fronds. It can be
propagated by division in spring.

Primula Pacific Series
(primrose)

☼ ◊ US Z 6–8 CAN Z 7

These low-growing perennials are
normally grown as biennials. Fragrant
flowers are produced in spring in
a range of colors, including white,
scarlet, violet, and yellow.

Pyracantha 'Teton'
(firethorn)

☼ ❋ ◊ US Z 6–9 CAN Z 7

The glossy leaves of this upright
evergreen shrub provide a long season
of interest. White flower clusters
appear in early summer, followed by
golden orange berries in autumn. Dead
growth should be pruned out in spring.

Pyrethrum ptarmiciflorum
'Silver Feather'

☼ ◊ US Z 9–11 CAN Z 9

Also sold as *Tanacetum*, this plant
has finely divided, bright silver leaves
that are eye-catchingly attractive. It
bears white and yellow, daisy-like
flowers in summer.

R

Rebutia marsoneri

☼ ◊ tender below 41°F (5°C)

A small, barrel-shaped cactus, this is
densely covered with golden yellow
flowers in early summer.

Rosa 'China Doll' (rose)
☼ ◗ US Z 5–9   CAN Z 6
This neat polyantha rose has a
spreading habit and produces clusters
of small, double, pearly pink flowers.

Rosa 'Flower Carpet' (rose)
☼ ◗ US Z 5–9   CAN Z 6
Hardy and robust, this rose's growth
is compact, requires little pruning,
and is free-flowering. This variety is
disease-resistant and produces cerise-
pink flowers throughout the summer.

Rosa 'Jeanne Lajoie' (rose)
☼ ◗ US Z 5–9   CAN Z 6
This rose bears blush-pink flowers. It
may be trained up a small trellis as a
miniature climber, or allowed to trail.

Rosa 'Red Cascade' (rose)
☼ ◗ US Z 5–9   CAN Z 6
This neat rose produces a profusion
of deep red flowers in summer. It is
excellent in a hanging basket.

Rosa 'Simplex' (rose)
☼ ◗ US Z 5–9   CAN Z 6
An outstanding, repeat-flowering
miniature rose, this cultivar has glossy,
dark green foliage and produces
abundant, elegant, tight buds that
open into clear pink flowers.

Rosa 'Sweet Magic' (rose)
☼ ◗ US Z 5–9   CAN Z 6
This striking variety produces clusters
of orange buds that become apricot as
they open into double flowers, then
slowly fade to a peachy yellow. 'Sweet
Magic' has been bred to be resistant
to disease and has a light fragrance.

Rosmarinus officinalis
'Severn Sea' (rosemary)
☼ ◗ US Z 8–10   CAN Z 9
This variety of rosemary is smaller
than most, making it ideal for
growing in a pot. It has spreading,
slightly arching branches and bright
blue flowers in late spring.

S

Salvia coccinea 'Coral Nymph'
☼ ✳ ◗ A
A deceptively delicate-looking plant,
this sturdy annual produces spikes
of salmon-pink, tubular flowers
throughout the summer.

Salvia farinacea 'Victoria'
☼ ✳ ◗ A
This perennial variety is usually
grown as an annual and bears masses
of deep violet-blue flower spikes.

Salvia officinalis 'Icterina' (sage)
☼ ✳ ◗ US Z 5–8   CAN Z 6
This variegated, green-and-gold variety
of culinary sage has as much flavor
as the plain green variety, but is less
hardy. 'Purpurascens' (purple sage)
is the purple-leaved variety.

Rosa 'Sweet Magic'

Sedum morganianum
(burro's tail)
☼ ◌ tender below 41–45°F (5–7°C)
An evergreen succulent, this bears long
tails of densely packed, blue-green
leaves and star-shaped flowers in spring
and summer. It should be handled with
care since its leaves fall off easily.

Soleirolia soleirolii
(baby's tears)
☼ ✸ ◗ T
The rampantly creeping habit of this
perennial, with its tiny, fresh green
leaves, makes it ideal for creating
a carpet of color in a pot. It is
evergreen in a frost-free climate.

Stachys lanata
(lamb's ears)
☼ ◗ US Z 4–9   CAN Z 5
This evergreen perennial has felted
silver leaves. In summer, spikes bear
tiny flowers. Old leaves should be cut
off to encourage fresh growth. It can
be propagated by division.

T

Tradescantia fluminensis
'Albovittata' (wandering Jew)
☼ ✸ ◗ tender below 50–61°F (10–16°C)
Usually grown as a houseplant, this
evergreen perennial will survive
outside in summer. This variety has
bright white-and-green variegations.

Trifolium repens 'Purpurascens'
(purple-leaved clover)
☼ ◗ US Z 4–8   CAN Z 5
A fast-growing perennial, this has
striking, variegated, usually four-
leaved foliage and white flowers.

Tropaeolum 'Salmon Baby'
(nasturtium)

☼ ✳ ◗ A

This variety of nasturtium produces
salmon-pink, semi-double flowers
above rich green, rounded leaves.

Tropaeolum 'Tom Thumb'
(nasturtium)

☼ ✳ ◗ A

This dwarf annual bears single flowers
in a range of colors, from cream,
through yellow and orange, to red.

Tulipa 'Angelique' (tulip)

☼ ◗ US Z 3–8   CAN Z 4a

A delightful, peony-like tulip with
double flowers in pale pink with dark
pink markings, this opens in full sun.

Tulipa 'Maureen' (tulip)

☼ ◗ US Z 3–8   CAN Z 4a

A creamy white, oval-shaped single
tulip, this flowers in late spring.

Tulipa 'Queen of Night' (tulip)

☼ ◗ US Z 3–8   CAN Z 4a

This striking tulip bears velvety, purple,
almost black flowers in late spring.

Tulipa 'Showwinner' (tulip)

☼ ◗ US Z 3–8   CAN Z 4a

This dwarf variety of tulip produces
vibrant scarlet flowers in early spring.

V

Verbena bonariensis
syn. *V. patagonica*

☼ ◗ US Z 5–9   CAN Z 6

A tall, stiffly branching perennial, this
produces small heads of intense violet-
blue flowers from summer to autumn.

Verbena bonariensis syn. *V. patagonica*

Verbena* × *hybrida

☼ ◗ A

There are many varieties of this
perennial available, which are usually
grown as annuals, in a wide range
of rich, vivid colors. 'Carousel'
has mauve and white flowers;
'Imagination' deep violet-blue;
the flower clusters of 'Peaches and
Cream' are salmon-pink, fading
to apricot, then pale yellow; 'Pink
Kleopatra' bears intense, magenta-
pink flowers, while the large
flowerheads of 'Pink Parfait' are
in two shades of pink; 'White
Kleopatra' has pure white flowers.

Viburnum tinus

✳ ✲ ◗ US Z 6–9   CAN Z 7

An invaluable evergreen shrub for
a shady site, this has leathery, oval
leaves. Clusters of pinkish white
flowers open from red buds in winter.

Vinca minor 'Variegata'
(lesser periwinkle)

☼ ✲ ◗ US Z 4–8   CAN Z 5

A trailing evergreen, this has
attractive, small, cream-and-green
leaves and, from early spring to
summer, violet-blue, star-like flowers.

Viola 'Bowles' Black'

☼ ✳ ◗ US Z 4–8   CAN Z 5

From summer to late autumn, this
perennial produces tiny, velvety,
almost black flowers with small but
prominent golden eyes.

Viola cornuta alba
(horned violet)

☼ ✳ ◗ US Z 6–9   CAN Z 7

In spring and summer, the perennial,
white horned violet has small, slightly
scented flowers held on upright stems
above glossy, green leaves. It may
have a late flush of flowers in autumn.

Viola* × *wittrockiana (pansy)

☼ ◗ A

A low-growing, spreading perennial
grown as an annual, varieties of this
plant flower in winter and spring, or
summer. Flower colors include red,
yellow, and blue, singles and bicolors.

Vitis vinifera 'Purpurea'
(purple-leaved grape)

☼ ✳ ◗ US Z 5–9   CAN Z 6

The leaves of this deciduous,
ornamental climber are gray-green in
spring, turning wine-red in summer,
and rich purple in autumn. Inedible
grapes are produced in summer.

Y

Yucca filamentosa
(Adam's needle)

☼ ◗ US Z 3–9   CAN Z 4a

The sharp, sword-like leaves of this
evergreen shrub are edged with fine,
curling threads. Mature plants
produce tall spires of creamy, bell-like
flowers from mid- to late summer.

INDEX

ACKNOWLEDGMENTS

AUTHOR'S ACKNOWLEDGMENTS

Grateful thanks are due first of all to Jean Goldberry and Louise Hampden for their contributions to the design of the arrangements. To art editors Emma Boys and Gurinder Purewall for their enthusiasm and attention to detail and to project editor Emma Lawson who, in addition to actually editing the book, worked so tirelessly in finding all the plants and containers. A particular thank you to her and Louise Hampden, too, for making the long days we spent planting up the arrangements so enjoyable. To Bob Collett of Petersham Nurseries who grew many of the plants for us, and tracked down others with unflagging enthusiasm and good humor. To Nick Lawrence and his team at Landscape Management who looked after the arrangements so well between planting and photography. To Matthew Ward and his team for the superb photographs. Finally, thanks as always to Tony for his support and optimism and for not minding the dirt under my nails.

PUBLISHER'S ACKNOWLEDGMENTS

Dorling Kindersley would like to thank the following: Bob Collett at Petersham Nursery for growing and supplying plants; Nick Lawrence, Anna Bartholomew, and their team at Landscape Management for looking after the planted-up containers; Martin Whitaker at Ginkgo Garden Centre for advice and for supplying plants; Avon Bulbs and Taylors for supplying bulbs; D. T. Brown, Dobies, Suttons, and Thompson & Morgan for supplying seeds; Evergreen Soil & Terracotta Ltd., Tendercare Nurseries, Dorney Court, Thorncroft Clematis Nursery, Orchard Dene Nurseries, Southern Plant Sales, and Cactus Heaven for supplying plants; the Palm Centre for the rental of *Chamaerops humilis*; Stuart and Joan Mungall at Patio for the rental of containers; Christopher Winder for the wooden topiary frame; Nick Hewitt for constructing boxes and sets; Hozelock for the micro-irrigation system; Fired Earth tiles for the loan of tiles; Fulham Palace Garden Centre for the rental of containers; Metalcraft Ltd. for the rental of railings; Travis Perkins for the flue liners; David Shelley, Chacasta Pritlove, and Anna Youle for their general assistance.

Photographer Matthew Ward

Photographer's assistants Al Deane, Karen Thomas

Hand models Steve Benjamin, Toby Heran, Katie Martin, Audrey Speitel

Illustrator Ann Winterbotham
Planting plan artworks Darren Hill

Container stylist Gilly Spargo

Editorial assistance Adèle Hayward

Design assistance Austin Barlow

Indexer Chris Bernstein
Proofreader Philip Parr

Picture researchers Christine Rista, Helen Stallion

Additional photography Peter Anderson, Steve Gorton, Dave King

PICTURE CREDITS

The publishers are grateful to the following photographers and picture libraries for permission to reproduce their photographs:

Key: *a* **above,** *b* **below,** *c* **center,** *l* **left,** *r* **right,** *t* **top**

Eric Crichton 128*t*;
Garden Picture Library Lynne Brotchie 126–127, Linda Burgess 31, Erika Craddock 59, John Glover 88*t*, Steven Wooster 92;
Jerry Harpur 91*l*, (Bourton House) 87*b*, (Susie Ind) 95*t*, (Phillip Watson, VA) 86*r*, (Beth Chatto) 138*t*;
Neil Holmes 95*b*;
Andrew Lawson 11;
Clive Nichols 127, (designer Anthony Noel) 91*r*, 94;
Hugh Palmer 10–11;
Photo Lamontagne 58–59, 84–85, 85, 86*l*, 101;
Royal Horticultural Society, Wisley W. Halliday 125*br*;
Elizabeth Whiting & Associates 30–31, 87*t*, 100–101.